Summary of a Workshop on the
Technology, Policy, and Cultural Dimensions of Biometric Systems

Kristen Batch, Lynette I. Millett, Joseph N. Pato, Editors

Whither Biometrics Committee

Computer Science and Telecommunications Board

Division on Engineering and Physical Sciences

NATIONAL RESEARCH COUNCIL
OF THE NATIONAL ACADEMIES

THE NATIONAL ACADEMIES PRESS
Washington, D.C.
www.nap.edu

THE NATIONAL ACADEMIES PRESS   500 Fifth Street, N.W.   Washington, DC 20001

NOTICE: The project that is the subject of this report was approved by the Governing Board of the National Research Council, whose members are drawn from the councils of the National Academy of Sciences, the National Academy of Engineering, and the Institute of Medicine. The members of the committee responsible for the report were chosen for their special competences and with regard for appropriate balance.

Support for this project was provided by the Defense Advanced Research Projects Agency (Award No. N00174-03-C-0074) and by the Central Intelligence Agency and the Department of Homeland Security with assistance from the National Science Foundation (Award No. IIS-0344584). Any opinions expressed in this material are those of the authors and do not necessarily reflect the views of the agencies and organizations that provided support for the project.

International Standard Book Number 0-309-10125-5

Cover designed by Jennifer M. Bishop.

Additional copies of this report are available from:

The National Academies Press
500 Fifth Street, N.W., Lockbox 285
Washington, DC 20055
800/624-6242
202/334-3313 (in the Washington metropolitan area)
http://www.nap.edu

Copyright 2006 by the National Academy of Sciences. All rights reserved.

Printed in the United States of America

THE NATIONAL ACADEMIES
Advisers to the Nation on Science, Engineering, and Medicine

The **National Academy of Sciences** is a private, nonprofit, self-perpetuating society of distinguished scholars engaged in scientific and engineering research, dedicated to the furtherance of science and technology and to their use for the general welfare. Upon the authority of the charter granted to it by the Congress in 1863, the Academy has a mandate that requires it to advise the federal government on scientific and technical matters. Dr. Ralph J. Cicerone is president of the National Academy of Sciences.

The **National Academy of Engineering** was established in 1964, under the charter of the National Academy of Sciences, as a parallel organization of outstanding engineers. It is autonomous in its administration and in the selection of its members, sharing with the National Academy of Sciences the responsibility for advising the federal government. The National Academy of Engineering also sponsors engineering programs aimed at meeting national needs, encourages education and research, and recognizes the superior achievements of engineers. Dr. Wm. A. Wulf is president of the National Academy of Engineering.

The **Institute of Medicine** was established in 1970 by the National Academy of Sciences to secure the services of eminent members of appropriate professions in the examination of policy matters pertaining to the health of the public. The Institute acts under the responsibility given to the National Academy of Sciences by its congressional charter to be an adviser to the federal government and, upon its own initiative, to identify issues of medical care, research, and education. Dr. Harvey V. Fineberg is president of the Institute of Medicine.

The **National Research Council** was organized by the National Academy of Sciences in 1916 to associate the broad community of science and technology with the Academy's purposes of furthering knowledge and advising the federal government. Functioning in accordance with general policies determined by the Academy, the Council has become the principal operating agency of both the National Academy of Sciences and the National Academy of Engineering in providing services to the government, the public, and the scientific and engineering communities. The Council is administered jointly by both Academies and the Institute of Medicine. Dr. Ralph J. Cicerone and Dr. Wm. A. Wulf are chair and vice chair, respectively, of the National Research Council.

www.national-academies.org

WHITHER BIOMETRICS COMMITTEE

JOSEPH N. PATO, Hewlett-Packard Labs, *Chair*
BOB BLAKLEY, IBM Tivoli Software
JEANETTE BLOMBERG, IBM Almaden Research Center
JOSEPH P. CAMPBELL, Massachusetts Institute of Technology, Lincoln Laboratory
GEORGE T. DUNCAN, Carnegie Mellon University
DELORES ETTER, U.S. Naval Academy*
GEORGE R. FISHER, Prudential-Wachovia (retired)
STEVEN P. GOLDBERG, Georgetown University Law Center
PETER T. HIGGINS, Higgins-Hermansen Group, LLC
PETER B. IMREY, Cleveland Clinic
ANIL K. JAIN, Michigan State University
GORDON LEVIN, The Walt Disney World Company
LAWRENCE D. NADEL, Mitretek Systems
JAMES L. WAYMAN, San Jose State University

Staff

LYNETTE I. MILLETT, Senior Program Officer
KRISTEN BATCH, Associate Program Officer
MARGARET MARSH HUYNH, Senior Program Assistant

---

*Dr. Etter resigned from the committee in November 2005 upon her appointment as assistant secretary, Research, Development, and Acquisition, U.S. Navy.

COMPUTER SCIENCE AND TELECOMMUNICATIONS BOARD

JOSEPH F. TRAUB, Columbia University, *Chair*
ERIC BENHAMOU, Benhamou Global Ventures, LLC
DAVID D. CLARK, Massachusetts Institute of Technology, *CSTB chair emeritus*
WILLIAM DALLY, Stanford University
MARK E. DEAN, IBM Almaden Research Center
DAVID J. DEWITT, University of Wisconsin, Madison
DEBORAH ESTRIN, University of California, Los Angeles
JOAN FEIGENBAUM, Yale University
KEVIN KAHN, Intel Corporation
JAMES KAJIYA, Microsoft Corporation
MICHAEL KATZ, University of California, Berkeley
RANDY H. KATZ, University of California, Berkeley
SARA KIESLER, Carnegie Mellon University
BUTLER W. LAMPSON, Microsoft Corporation, *CSTB member emeritus*
TERESA H. MENG, Stanford University
TOM M. MITCHELL, Carnegie Mellon University
FRED B. SCHNEIDER, Cornell University
WILLIAM STEAD, Vanderbilt University
ANDREW J. VITERBI, Viterbi Group, LLC
JEANNETTE M. WING, Carnegie Mellon University

RICHARD E. ROWBERG, Acting Director
JON EISENBERG, Acting Associate Director
KRISTEN BATCH, Associate Program Officer
JENNIFER M. BISHOP, Program Associate
JANET BRISCOE, Manager, Program Operations
RENEE HAWKINS, Financial Associate
MARGARET MARSH HUYNH, Senior Program Assistant
HERBERT S. LIN, Senior Scientist
LYNETTE I. MILLETT, Senior Program Officer
JANICE SABUDA, Senior Program Assistant
TED SCHMITT, Program Officer
GLORIA WESTBROOK, Senior Program Assistant
BRANDYE WILLIAMS, Staff Assistant

For more information on CSTB, see its Web site at <http://www.cstb.org>, write to CSTB, National Research Council, 500 Fifth Street, N.W., Washington, DC 20001, call (202) 334-2605, or e-mail the CSTB at cstb@nas.edu.

Preface

Biometrics—the automatic identification or identity verification of human individuals on the basis of physiological and behavioral characteristics—is receiving much attention from many quarters. Promoted as a means to combat terrorism, to increase security, to boost efficiency, and to lessen inconvenience, biometrics is being considered, developed, and deployed in corporations, government agencies, and nonprofit institutions. Questions persist, however, about the effectiveness of biometric security measures, biometric systems' usability and manageability along with their appropriateness in widely varying contexts, the effects of federal privacy policy on use and deployment, and the social impact of such technologies.

In 2003 the Committee on Authentication Technologies and Their Privacy Implications issued the report *Who Goes There? Authentication Through the Lens of Privacy.* Biometric technologies were one of several authentication technologies considered in that report. Subsequent to its publication, the Computer Science and Telecommunications Board held several discussions with various federal agencies interested in biometrics. Jonathon Phillips (then at the Defense Advanced Research Projects Agency [DARPA]), Gary Strong (then at the Department of Homeland Security [DHS]), and Andrew Kirby (of the Central Intelligence Agency [CIA]) were active participants in stimulating the discussions and moving them forward. The discussions resulted in agreement to undertake a comprehensive assessment of biometrics that examines current capabilities, future possibilities, and the role of government in their development. Funding for the project was obtained from DARPA and from the CIA and DHS with assistance from the National Science Foundation. The Whither Biometrics Committee was appointed to conduct the study.

This report is the outcome of the first stages of the committee's work, which culminated in a public workshop organized by the committee and attended by members of industry, government, and academia. Held on March 15 and 16, 2005, in Washington, D.C., the workshop featured a variety of participants invited to present their views on issues surrounding biometric technologies and systems (see Appendix A for the workshop agenda). Five panels were organized, and each panelist gave a short presentation that addressed the theme of the panel. Each panel session was followed by extensive discussion involving all of the workshop participants and moderated by a committee member. This report is the committee's summary of the panelists' presentations and the ensuing discussions.

Although the summary is based on presentations and discussion at the workshop, the participants' comments do not necessarily reflect the views of the committee, nor does the summary present findings or recommendations of the National Research Council. In fact, the committee took care in writing this report simply to summarize the discussions and to avoid any bias or appearance of bias in favor of one opinion or another. The committee limited itself to recording the overall sense of each individual panel session and did not attempt to distill sentiments across panels. Further, this summary is not intended to be an outline of the committee's final report; topics that were not discussed at the workshop are not mentioned, however important they might be.

In the second stage of the study, the committee will analyze the information gathered in the workshop and summarized here, along with information and input from other experts and related studies. This analysis phase will deliver a final report (planned for release in 2006) with findings and recommendations from the committee.

The Whither Biometrics Committee consists of 14 members from industry and academia who are experts in different aspects of distributed systems, computer security, biometrics (of various flavors), systems engineering, human factors, and statistics, as well as in computer science and engineering (see Appendix B for committee and staff biographies).

The committee thanks the many individuals who contributed to its work, including the project sponsors that enabled this activity. It appreciates the panelists' willingness to address the questions posed to them and is grateful for their insights. It further wishes to recognize the energetic participation of the workshop attendees as a group. Their active engagement stimulated a more robust discussion than might have been expected. Additionally, the reviewers of the draft summary report provided insightful and constructive comments that contributed significantly to its clarity.

The committee is particularly grateful to the CSTB staff for their work. Lynette Millett, Senior Program Officer, serves as the study director and has been instrumental in guiding this project from concept to practice with grace, humor, and aplomb. Kristen Batch went well beyond the call of duty in preparing the draft report for review. Margaret Huynh has been ably coordinating logistics for meetings and providing administrative support to the committee between meetings. She and Gloria Westbrook provided excellent staff support during the workshop. Thanks also to Janet Briscoe, who provided oversight for the workshop, and to the editorial staff, Susan Maurizi and Liz Fikre, in the Division on Engineering and Physical Sciences.

Joe Pato, *Chair*
Whither Biometrics Committee

Acknowledgment of Reviewers

This report has been reviewed in draft form by individuals chosen for their diverse perspectives and technical expertise, in accordance with procedures approved by the National Research Council's (NRC's) Report Review Committee. The purpose of this independent review is to provide candid and critical comments that will assist the institution in making its published report as sound as possible and to ensure that the report meets institutional standards for objectivity, evidence, and responsiveness to the study charge. The review comments and draft manuscript remain confidential to protect the integrity of the deliberative process. We wish to thank the following individuals for their review of this report:

Vijayakumar Bhagavatula, Carnegie Mellon University,
Tora K. Bikson, RAND Corporation,
Austin Hicklin, Mitretek Systems,
Wendy Kellogg, IBM,
Sara Kiesler, Carnegie Mellon University,
James Matey, Sarnoff Corporation,
K.A. Taipale, Center for Advanced Studies in Science and Technology Policy, and
Andrew Viterbi, Viterbi Group, LLC.

Although the reviewers listed above have provided many constructive comments and suggestions, they were not asked to endorse the conclusions or recommendations, nor did they see the final draft of the report before its release. The review of this report was overseen by Stephen Kent of BBN Technologies. Appointed by the National Research Council, he was responsible for making certain that an independent examination of this report was carried out in accordance with institutional procedures and that all review comments were carefully considered. Responsibility for the final content of this report rests entirely with the authoring committee and the institution.

Contents

1	OVERVIEW OF WORKSHOP DISCUSSIONS	1
2	SUMMARY OF PANEL SESSIONS AND PRESENTATIONS	5

APPENDIXES
A	Workshop Agenda	35
B	Biosketches of Committee Members	40

WHAT IS CSTB?   47

1

Overview of Workshop Discussions

This report summarizes a workshop on the technology, policy, and cultural dimensions of biometrics systems held March 15 and 16, 2005, in Washington, D.C., under the auspices of the Whither Biometrics Committee. Several items should be kept in mind when reading this report:

- The workshop focused on a subset of areas that the committee believed would provide a basis for its work during the remaining study period. There are areas of direct relevance to the study that are missing from the workshop agenda, either because of time constraints or because the panelists chose to address different areas. (For example, some application domains were not discussed explicitly, although it should be clear from the context when an issue applies to biometric systems broadly and when it applies to a particular system.) The committee plans to gather input on those domains in subsequent activities; feedback and additional input from readers of this report are welcome.
- Given the diverse backgrounds of participants at the workshop, a variety of technologies and measures were discussed, ranging from fingerprints to facial recognition to DNA. While the applicability of high-level principles and systems considerations will change depending on a number of factors (for example, latent fingerprints can be captured long after a person has left the area, whereas a voiceprint disappears without a recording device available to capture it in real time), this report does not attempt to tease apart those considerations in detail. The committee's final report is expected to be a much more elaborated synthesis and analysis of what can be generalized about biometrics and will incorporate aspects of the workshop's discussions as well as additional input received over the course of the study.
- The committee has chosen not to extend the discussions in this first-phase report, instead reserving that task for the final report. Consequently, this report does not provide a free-standing overview of the current state of biometrics technology, biometrics research, current application domains (some of which were not touched on at this workshop), or anything other than the views expressed at this particular workshop. For readability and to promote understanding, background material on some of the topics raised has been interspersed with the record of presentations and discussions.

Listed below are some of the main themes arising from each panel session. The themes are not conclusions or findings of the committee; they are ideas extracted from each panel that seem to be the main thrusts of each discussion. Each panel session discussion is more fully elaborated in Chapter 2.

SESSION 1: SCIENTIFIC AND TECHNICAL CHALLENGES FOR BIOMETRIC TECHNOLOGIES AND SYSTEMS, INCLUDING SYSTEM INTEGRATION, ARCHITECTURE, AND CONTEXTS OF USE

In Session 1, participants from industry, government, and academic research centers discussed the state of the art of biometric systems, the current bottlenecks, and areas where performance could be improved. Among the different types of biometrics, three were highlighted by the panelists—fingerprint, iris, and face—as being those accepted by the International Civil Aviation Organization for use in border-crossing documents. All panelists agreed that biometric systems cannot be made perfect—that is, the focus should be on how to evaluate and reduce, rather than eliminate, error rates. The challenges relevant in varying degrees to all biometric systems were grouped into three categories by the panelists, with primary emphasis during this discussion given to the first category of challenges.

- Improving the accuracy of biometric technologies and related performance evaluations through research on sensor resolution and ergonomics, algorithms and techniques for biometric fusion, characteristics of biometric feature spaces, and scientific methods to better quantify biometric systems' performance under realistic conditions.
- Systematically and thoughtfully integrating biometric systems with other security systems.
- Promoting interoperability of biometric systems, especially internationally, through a framework of standards, test methodologies, and independent evaluations.

SESSION 2: MEASUREMENT, STATISTICS, TESTING, AND EVALUATION

Session 2 explored issues surrounding the measurement, statistics, testing, and evaluation of biometrics and biometric systems. It should be noted that statistical analysis in the context of biometric systems is and can be employed for a range of purposes, including assessments of the underlying technology, analysis of user behavior, data mining, and so on. Indeed, such issues were discussed throughout the workshop in several different contexts. Questions raised for this panel included these: Do biometric systems work? What is meant by "work" in the context of a biometrics system? *What* is being measured, tested, and evaluated, and how can confidence in the experiments be created? The panelists presented a range of perspectives on these issues, from broad explorations of the nature of experimentation and representative populations to discussions of specific evaluation regimens and real-world deployment at a major international airport. Several overarching themes arose:

- Evaluating biometric systems serves three purposes: to guide and support research and development, to assess the readiness of a system for deployment, and to monitor performance of a system in the field.
- As in many other domains, appropriate experimental design and solid statistical underpinnings are needed to produce effective testing and evaluation regimes. There is no one-size-fits-all solution, given the many types of systems that are deployed.

- Data and data selection choices, which include understanding the reference and expected user populations, can have a large impact on the accuracy and effectiveness of testing and evaluation.

SESSION 3: LEGISLATIVE, POLICY, HUMAN, AND CULTURAL FACTORS

In Session 3 panelists were asked to address the legal, policy, social, and cultural aspects of biometric systems, as well as the broad implications for society of the collection and use of biometric data in different contexts at both national and international levels. Major threads of presentations and discussions at this session included the following:

- Three different modes of identification evidence—mitochondrial DNA, facial recognition, and latent fingerprints—were discussed in relation to "general acceptance" and "scientific validity"—two legal standards for the admissibility of evidence in a court of law.
- Lessons for biometric system security were drawn from the current uses of Social Security numbers (SSNs) and the growing incidence of identity fraud. The proposition of a new law restricting the sale and disclosure of biometric identifiers was actively debated.
- The meaning of "privacy" in relation to the use of biometrics technologies was discussed in terms of legal principles and some preliminary public opinion survey research.
- Issues related to the collection and use of data generated by biometric technologies and associated fair information practices were discussed in relation to an earlier study on the use of radio-frequency identification tags (RFIDs) and access cards in the private sector.
- The international legal and cultural dimensions of privacy were discussed, including their implications for the use of biometrics.

SESSION 4: SCENARIOS AND APPLICATIONS

Session 4 participants were asked to discuss the impact of different application contexts on the performance of biometric systems and to describe general characteristics of successfully deployed biometric systems. Other topics covered in this session included approaches to the fusion of multiple biometrics and methods for integrating biometrics into particular system contexts and environments. Among the themes that emerged during the discussion were the following:

- The challenges identified for biometric identity management applications will vary depending on the application requirements, system scale, and the security environment.
- Nontechnical factors such as human factors and user training can have significant impacts on biometric system performance.
- Standards and interoperability are important for better system performance and the global use of biometric systems.

SESSION 5: TECHNICAL AND POLICY ASPECTS OF INFORMATION SHARING AND COOPERATION

Session 5 panelists were asked to discuss a variety of issues related to biometric data sharing, including technical challenges as they relate to synchronicity and connectivity of data on the one hand

and to security and privacy of data on the other hand; policy considerations for sharing biometric data between agencies; and practical considerations of standards development and cross-jurisdictional cooperation. The following are some of the topics covered in this session:

- Newly established and long-standing biometric data sharing applications at the state, national, and international level were described in the contexts of military defense, law enforcement, and immigration. Systems discussed included the Automated Biometric Identification System (ABIS), the Criminal Alien Identification System (CAIS), the Integrated Automated Fingerprint Identification System (IAFIS), and the United States Visitor and Immigrant Status Indicator Technology (US-VISIT) program.
- Technical and policy challenges related to information sharing among large-scale biometric systems were addressed, including data integrity and procedural analysis, consolidation of biometric information, and integration of databases.
- Broader policy challenges of biometric information sharing also were discussed, including (1) the importance of evaluating biometric systems based on their context, purpose, and the policies they serve; (2) establishing criteria to determine the usefulness of data for decision making; and (3) instituting careful procedures for maintaining and sharing digital records.

2

Summary of Panel Sessions and Presentations

SESSION 1: SCIENTIFIC AND TECHNICAL CHALLENGES FOR BIOMETRIC TECHNOLOGIES AND SYSTEMS, INCLUDING SYSTEM INTEGRATION, ARCHITECTURE, AND CONTEXTS OF USE

Panelists: Jean-Christophe Fondeur, James Matey, Sharath Pankanti, Jonathon Phillips, and David Scott
Moderator: Anil Jain

In Session 1, participants from industry, government, and academic research centers discussed the state of the art of biometric systems, the current bottlenecks, and areas where performance could be improved. Among the different types of biometrics, three were highlighted by the panelists—fingerprint, iris, and face—as being those accepted by the International Civil Aviation Organization for use in border-crossing documents.[1] All panelists agreed that biometric systems cannot be made perfect—that is, the focus should be on how to evaluate and reduce, rather than eliminate, error rates. The challenges relevant in varying degrees to all biometric systems were grouped in three categories by the panelists, with primary emphasis during this discussion given to the first category of challenges.

- Improving the accuracy of biometric technologies and related performance evaluations through research on sensor resolution and ergonomics, algorithms and techniques for biometric fusion, characteristics of biometric feature spaces, and scientific methods to better quantify biometric systems' performance under realistic conditions.
- Systematically and thoughtfully integrating biometric systems with other security systems.
- Promoting interoperability of biometric systems, especially internationally, through a framework of standards, test methodologies, and independent evaluations.

Underlying many of the scientific and technical challenges for biometric technologies and systems is the need to reduce the error and variability that can be introduced at various stages. The

---

[1] While these particular types of biometrics were highlighted by these panelists, there are scientific and technical challenges across a range of biometrics, including non-image-based measures such as voice recognition. The committee's final report will aim to incorporate and extend the discussions at this workshop and to include biometric measures and systems that were not specifically mentioned at this event.

sources of error begin with insufficient distinguishing detail in the biometric identifiers themselves (such as faint fingerprint ridges) and extend to variability in their presentations to a sensing instrument (which, depending on what is being measured and how, may result from injury, changing lighting conditions, or the aging process). The capture of the biometric identifiers by the sensors is affected both by the human interaction with the sensor (such as assisted vs. nonassisted sample capture and cooperative vs. noncooperative system users) and by the precision of the acquisition device itself. The quality of the information extracted from the sensor and used in the subsequent matching process can vary as well. The metric used in the matching process to measure similarities may be faulty or lack sufficient information to determine a match or a mismatch. Furthermore, to understand how the various stages of the data acquisition and processing sequence affect the end performance of the biometric system and how they can be improved, each stage needs to be modeled independently as well as in different system architectures.

Biometrics and Accuracy

To increase the information captured by the biometric system and to facilitate matching, including the ability to discriminate between genuine and imposter matches, participants suggested that sensor improvements could involve higher resolution and a higher signal-to-noise ratio (SNR). In addition, sensors that collect multiple biometrics within one device or system may offer improvements with respect to a range of characteristics such as accuracy and efficiency and accommodation of a broader population. Current research in this area aims to make multiple low-resolution images from video surveillance systems usable for facial recognition. An example was given of a system that uses several different cameras to track the location of a person in a room, with one of the cameras controlled by the location of the person's head. Such a system can log all the people who have been in a room and capture the frontal images that are best suited to facial recognition at higher resolution.

Given that users of biometric systems may not be familiar with the technology, the ergonomics of the sensor and associated data capture hardware may affect the biometric information that is collected. To improve results, some participants suggested that user interaction must be either intuitive or minimized to the point that there is little, or no, interaction with the acquisition device. The prototype discussed at the workshop for on-the-move iris recognition allows iris images to be captured while the individual is walking past the sensor. This approach aims to minimize the acquisition constraints by expanding the standoff distance, or the distance of the acquisition system and the camera illumination from the subject, and the capture volume, or the area in which the biometric may be captured within a particular length of time.[2] However, additional improvements in algorithms will be required to further minimize these constraints as well as reduce orientation requirements that currently require a direct gaze into the camera.

Continued algorithm development and better fusion of biometrics will generate more information to aid in the matching process. Though algorithms are continuing to improve and to process more information, additional research will be needed in coping with the variability of information over time—a consequence of the human aging process—especially for the processing of children and particularly for new biometric modes, such as three-dimensional facial recognition. For biometric fusion, panelists suggested potentially good combinations, such as face and finger, finger

---

[2] The performance of the off-the-shelf iris recognition system described at the workshop, the LG-3000, includes a standoff of 10 cm, a capture volume of 0.04 liters, or 2 cm * 2 cm * 10 cm, within 3-10 seconds, and requires stationary use. In contrast, the on-the-move iris recognition prototype increases the camera standoff to 3 m and illumination by 1 m, capture volume expands to 10 liters, or 60 cm * 30 cm * 5 cm, within 0.05 seconds, and permits a walking speed of 1 m per second.

and iris, and face and iris. Research in this area also includes mosaicking templates[3] that allow for the integration of multiple acquisitions of a biometric to enhance its representation.

In addition to improving the collection, processing, and integration of biometric information, panelists also underscored the importance of understanding more about biometrics feature spaces, including determining how many independent dimensions there are for each unimodal biometric, how many are required to determine distinctness, and variation in feature space dimensionality across different biometric modes. Biostatistical tools and processes could also be helpful in determining the effectiveness of dimensions in creating and using representative but smaller test populations and in understanding changes in biometric identifiers over time.

Biometrics and Performance

Though many panelists believed that the performance issues surrounding biometric technologies are tractable, they agreed that resolving these issues will require a systems approach rather than a focus on individual sensors and recognition algorithms. This approach calls for collaboration by those involved with different stages of a biometric application and the integration of modalities, sensors, and application subcontexts—for example, the integration of liveliness detection with signal quality assessment—to promote better system decisions. In general, effective system integration was considered to be necessary for improving accuracy and performance.

To evaluate and to compare the current accuracy and improvements in accuracy of biometric systems, a more scientific approach to biometric performance research was suggested. Participants recognized the progression of biometric research, from the early approach of selective performance tests to the recent use of more robust approaches to technology evaluation, which can aid in organizing and comparing the results of the system under evaluation.[4] But some panelists stressed the importance of more systematic research. Additional progress could be made by the more systematic use of control groups (for example, testing a new algorithm against a control algorithm), by establishing confidence intervals to indicate statistical significance to achieve better consistency across studies,[5] and by aiming for repeatability of studies to verify performance improvements through independent evaluations. Various suggestions that were offered to develop a research agenda are described in Box 2.1.

Biometrics and Security

The panelists agreed that biometrics should not stand alone in security practices but should be systematically and thoughtfully integrated with other security features. Noting that a biometric (for example, a fingerprint or an iris pattern) itself is not secret, panelists observed that it is necessary to consider its integration with other security mechanisms such as encryption and/or smart cards. Integrity mechanisms employing encryption, for example, are required to provide continuity of authentication for the duration of a session, something that biometrics alone cannot provide for this sort of application. One suggestion was to pursue a holistic approach for integrating biometrics into a

---

[3] Anil K. Jain and Arun Ross, 2002, "Fingerprint mosaicking," Proceedings of IEEE International Conference on Acoustics, Speech, and Signal Processing (ICASSP), Orlando, Fla., May 13-17.

[4] Some formal technology evaluations conducted by the National Institute of Standards and Technology (NIST), for example, include the Face Recognition Grand Challenge (FRGC), the Iris Challenge Evaluation (ICE), the Speaker Recognition Evaluation (SRE), and the Minutiae Operability Exchange Test (MINEX04).

[5] This would be helpful when replicating experiments with different data sets and to verify the correctness of testing methodologies.

> **BOX 2.1**
> **Suggestions for Improving Biometrics Research Endeavors**
>
> Various suggestions were offered to improve biometrics research:
>
> - Improve the consistency of review policies by using a peer-review process (such as is used for journals) to facilitate repeatability, documentation of experiments, and executability.
> - Provide access to large data sets and different types of data, such as multimodal data, to measure performance improvements and find ways to increase the amount of data used in biometric performance studies.[1]
> - Develop challenge problems to guide academic research and to create a baseline for comparisons and independent evaluations.
> - Increase the documentation of government-funded and -proposed research (see Session 2 for additional discussion).
>
> ---
> [1] It was also noted that studies outlining new performance techniques may not require data for testing until later stages.

security system and to consider employing techniques like the Common Criteria certification approach.[6]

Biometrics and Interoperability

An international framework to support the worldwide interoperability of biometrics requires the creation of standards, test methodologies, and independent evaluations. Interoperability challenges described during the workshop include identity documents issued in one country using the system of a particular vendor, which must be accessible in other countries using different systems of different vendors. Standards are needed to facilitate this interchangeability, but it was noted that they will not solve all the problems, because they often involve compromises among the different and sometimes competing interest groups that are involved in any given standards process. Incompatibilities in the interpretation of standards require evaluation tests to be conducted. In addition, it was suggested that many operational pilot programs should also include interoperability testing in multiple countries to verify that systems will be compatible (see Session 4 for more discussion).

SESSION 2: MEASUREMENT, STATISTICS, TESTING, AND EVALUATION

Panelists: George Doddington, Michele Freadman, Patrick Grother, Austin Hicklin, and Nell Sedransk
Moderator: Joseph Campbell

Session 2 explored issues surrounding the measurement, statistics, testing, and evaluation of biometrics and biometric systems. It should be noted that statistical analysis in the context of biometric systems is employed for a range of purposes, including assessments of the underlying

---
[6] For more information, see <http://csrc.nist.gov/cc/>.

technology, analysis of user behavior, data mining, and so on. Indeed, such issues were discussed throughout the workshop in several different contexts. Questions raised for this panel included these: Do biometric systems work? What is meant by "work" in the context of a biometrics system? What is being measured, tested, and evaluated, and how can confidence in the experiments be created? The panelists presented a range of perspectives on these issues, from broad explorations of the nature of experimentation and representative populations to discussions of specific evaluation regimens and real-world deployment at a major international airport (see Box 2.2). Several overarching themes arose:

- Evaluating biometric systems serves three purposes: to guide and support research and development, to assess the readiness of a system for deployment, and to monitor performance of a system in the field.
- As in many other domains, appropriate experimental design and solid statistical underpinnings are needed to produce effective testing and evaluation regimes. There is no one-size-fits-all solution, given the range of types of systems that are deployed.
- Data and data selection choices, which include understanding the reference and expected user populations, can have a large impact on the accuracy and effectiveness of testing and evaluation.

BOX 2.2
Early Biometrics System Deployment at an Airport

One panelist described the evaluation of different biometric technologies for several operational deployments, as well as the design of a future biometric system for controlling access to Boston's air transportation system. At the time of this workshop the biometric systems deployed by Massport, the responsible government agency, included an ultrasonic fingerprint reader at the regional airport and hand geometry readers in the administration building. The planned system for Logan airport, soon to be deployed, takes a layered approach, following Secure Identification Display Area (SIDA) procedures, and uses a proximity card, a personal identification number (PIN), and a fingerprint reader. The panelist emphasized the importance of examining an organization's expectations of a biometric system and what such a system could accomplish, in particular recognizing that biometrics alone would not solve security concerns, and stressed the importance of initial enrollments and the need to educate both enrollment administrators and system users to acquire high-quality enrollments. Educating employees was also critical to gaining acceptance for the technology. To promote the success of the Massport system, the importance of addressing concerns about the technology as they arose was noted. A general plan was also proactively put in place, increasing administrative staff to assist with any problems or issues that might arise during the initial deployment period.

Purpose and Goals of Evaluation

Biometric technologies and systems are commonly used for security purposes and for the sake of convenience. One application of biometrics is to gain a privilege (for example, access to buildings or other resources). Another class of biometric applications is forensics and intelligence gathering—specifically, the use of biometrics to validate the identity of a person who does not want to be identified. Both classes of applications should be kept in mind when exploring testing and evaluation approaches. For both, the major challenge is obtaining a biometric trait sufficiently distinctive to determine differences between people in the face of measurement variability across multiple presentations of the user to the system, which may vary greatly in time and circumstances (including degree of user cooperation), and in the face of possible attempts to manipulate and/or circumvent the system by imposters.

There are many types of biometrics that might be used in a system. Some biometrics are based on physical characteristics, such as fingerprints, hand geometry, facial features, and so on, whereas others are based more on performance or behavior, such as signatures and speech. Biometric measurements have a range of variabilities, including physical variabilities (due, for example, to aging or trauma) and physiological variabilities, such as emotional or metabolic changes. Additional variability may be due to idiosyncrasies of the population (see Box 2.3). All of these types of variability, and others, pose challenges for collecting a corpus (training set) representing the problem space and for ensuring that quantitative indices of performance are sufficiently precise. They also can be sources of error when considering a distribution of subjects for enrollment and verification. The challenges associated with data and data selection are described further in a later section.

BOX 2.3
Sheep and Goats

The performance challenges to biometric systems due to variability, particularly in the recognition of different speakers within a population, are a well-recognized problem within the speaker recognition community. Variability among speakers has led some researchers to class them as "sheep," "goats," "lambs," and "wolves." Sheep represent the largest portion of the population—their performance is both predictable and reliably recognized by the system. Goats are fewer in number—their performance in the system is unpredictable and not reliably recognized, often resulting in detection errors. Lambs and wolves are easily confused with others and can result in false matches. The characteristics of lambs are easy to imitate. Wolves, on the other hand, can imitate others easily.

---
[1] For more, see George Doddington, Walter Liggett, Alvin Martin, Mark Przybocki, and Douglas Reynolds, 1998, "Sheep, goats, lambs and wolves: A statistical analysis of speaker performance in the NIST 1998 speaker recognition evaluation," Proceedings of the 5th International Conference on Spoken Language Processing, November.

Why Evaluate?

What is the reason for evaluation and testing of a biometric system? At a high level, it was suggested, evaluation serves three purposes: (1) to guide and support research and development by, among other things, identifying important dimensions of variability and providing feedback on what works and what does not; (2) to assess the readiness of a system for deployment and to provide a framework for characterizing performance as a function of variability in a given system; and (3) to monitor performance of a system in the field, which includes characterizing system performance in terms of the failure mechanisms and identifying technical challenges that can feed back to research and development.

Over time, tension may result between research and applications. For research, the requirement is to represent core technical challenges in a very distilled way that separates the technical issues from numerous application/operational issues. As application and operational issues arise, they may complicate and obscure the core research challenges. At the same time, if evaluation is needed to assess readiness, then the prediction of a system's performance in the field may be based on what the system achieved on a corpus of evaluation data. Accurate predictions can be a challenge.

The Role of Technology

Regardless of the specific reasons for evaluating a given system, ultimately the role of technology—in this case of a biometric system—is to enable accurate and responsible decision making. At heart, a panelist suggested, all practical biometric applications are "detection" applications: The application seeks to assert that an identity is known or is not known. It was suggested that this assertion can be formulated in terms of a probability—namely, is the probability of the identity hypothesis, given the data, above a certain threshold? Participants acknowledged that answering this question is not solely a technical matter. Policy matters as well. What are the criteria on which this judgment is based? What are the prior probabilities—that is, Is anything known about the probabilities associated with the population using the technology? How will the answer that the technology is attempting to provide weigh into the ultimate decision making? Policy and adjudication mechanisms are needed in addition to what the technologists and technological systems can offer. Participants observed that the technical and policy components of decision making must inform and provide feedback to each other.

Experimental Design

Participants noted that good experimental design is important in evaluating systems and selecting evaluation data and that many of the issues that arise are not specific to biometrics. Data selection issues need to be acknowledged up front rather than being hidden or elided in the evaluation of systems. Issues of proper data use were also raised, such as including all data in the test evaluation. Removal of poor quality data from the test could have the effect of filtering out problems that would occur with real data and might produce overoptimistic assessments of system performance. Additionally, the operational and evaluation data need to be kept separate to prevent developers from tuning their systems to known evaluation data sets in preparation for testing.

Some challenges specific to evaluating biometric systems are specific to each of the many types of systems that are deployed. As one panelist noted, evaluating "operational fingerprint identification systems on a large scale" is a specific challenge—changing any of the characteristics mentioned in that phrase changes the evaluation process. Another challenge relates to what is known as ground truth and the process of determining whether there is a matching error. Fingerprint identification may involve working with latent fingerprint examiners, who, as is well known, can make errors. Testing also needs to be done for system vulnerabilities, and distinctions should be made between active and passive imposters. Additionally, it was noted that a one-size-fits-all approach to testing might not be feasible, because the intended use for the system and the type of application might have an impact on the referent population and on the types of data necessary to evaluate the system. It was suggested that layering the overall problem into general problems, biometric-related problems, specific biometric modalities issues, and so on would generally be helpful. One suggestion was to layer the problem so as to address all the generic problems first (such as defining the general-purpose evaluation and data selection and corpus) and then to address problems relating to the specific biometric technologies and modalities in use. Of course, the generic and the specific may not always be easily separable.

Impact of Data Selection on Testing and Evaluation

Data selection is central to effective evaluation approaches. That which can be learned from a data set that is not representative of the population of interest is of limited, if any, value.[7] The degree of similarity among different elements in a population is a related concern and must be considered when establishing a representative population sample and incorporating appropriate gradation and other challenges into test scenarios. Biometric tests are almost universally based on "opportunity" samples, testing whatever volunteers happen to be available. It might be possible to develop "judgment" samples chosen in some systematic way to represent population variation. The application of statistical methods to evaluations in the biometrics domain would seem viable, provided that the methods are well designed and the samples are representative.[8]

One panelist argued that large quantities of operational data are needed for testing. While most systems do not archive all of their data, much could be learned from the analysis of data that are routinely discarded if they are collected and stored (for example, retaining the information that a person had to make three attempts before the system recognized him or her, and the biometric images or signals associated with those repeated attempts). Data also drive how thresholds are set for biometric systems. Thresholds are predicated on what is known about the distributions of imposters and genuine subjects. Developing an infrastructure to extract operational data from devices may be helpful, but techniques for anonymization and privacy protection along with authentication, where appropriate, will also be needed. It was suggested that a combination of interfaces, infrastructures, audit trails, metadata, and data formats is needed. Despite the difficulty of gathering data from subjects, participants were skeptical about the use of synthetic data (created through morphing and other techniques) for testing a system for deployment but allowed that such data might be useful in the early stages of research and development testing.

Data distributions also vary by collection characteristics as well as population characteristics. For instance, data compiled by trained collectors in a controlled environment who aim to gather perfect samples from willing participants will likely be less variable than data collected in operational field tests under chaotic conditions by untrained collectors or from uncooperative participants. Additionally, the two kinds of data—controlled versus operational—also have different uses. For purposes of research and development, controlled laboratory data might be more useful—for example, in order to assess the sensitivities of one's algorithms. However, for testing purposes, operational data are preferable.

Quality

In some biometric systems, annotations that indicate the quality of a particular sample can be used. For example, some data formats for face, finger, and iris have fields that allow a quality metric to be inserted. This metric can be used to guide what sort of analysis might be needed or, at

---

[7] One example was of a data set collected in an Ohio prison—not only was the collection process very controlled, but the population was homogeneous (primarily young and male) compared with the general population. Another example addressing the issue of collection involved two different populations but used the same fingerprint scanners and the same software: one set of data was collected by the border patrol (primarily from Mexican illegal immigrants) and the other one was collected in an office environment (from people trying to get border-crossing cards). These systems were orders of magnitude apart in terms of error rates, presumably because the two populations from which the data were being collected had very different motivations.

[8] It was noted that statistical error bars on data will indicate the degree of error only if the data reflect the population. If the data do not reflect the population, then the error bars will not have any bearing on the true magnitude of error.

enrollment, to ask that the sample be collected again. It can also be used in aggregate to assess or monitor the overall quality of the collected data. For example, if enrollment is being done at multiple stations, system operators can learn about the average quality on, for instance, Mondays, or in the afternoons. Much of this falls under traditional quality control and analysis.[9] How best to use such a quality metric, what standards it might be useful for, and what it actually means are being discussed in the biometrics community.

SESSION 3: LEGISLATIVE, POLICY, HUMAN, AND CULTURAL FACTORS

Panelists: Tora Bikson, David Kaye, Lisa Nelson, and Peter Swire
Moderator: Jeanette Blomberg

In Session 3 panelists were asked to address the legal, policy, social, and cultural aspects of biometric systems, as well as the implications for the collection and use of biometric data in different contexts at both the national and international levels. Five main themes emerged during this session:

- Three different modes of identification evidence—mitochondrial DNA, facial recognition, and latent fingerprints—were discussed in relation to "general acceptance" and "scientific validity"—two legal standards for the admissibility of evidence in a court of law.
- Lessons for biometric system security were drawn from the current use of SSNs and the growing incidence of identity fraud. The proposition of a new law restricting the sale and disclosure of biometric identifiers was debated.
- The meaning of "privacy" in relation to the use of biometrics technologies was discussed in terms of legal principles and some preliminary public opinion survey research.
- Issues related to the collection and use of data generated by biometric technologies and associated fair information practices were discussed in relation to an earlier study on the use of RFIDs and access cards in the private sector.
- The international legal and cultural dimensions of privacy were discussed, including their implications for the use of biometrics.

Admissibility of Biometric Identification Evidence

Two standards in common use for the admissibility of evidence in American trial courts,[10] typically called "general acceptance" and "scientific validity," were discussed and later applied to three different biometric identification modes. In practice, which of these standards applies varies by jurisdiction. The first standard, "general acceptance," originated in *Frye v. United States*, a District of Columbia Court of Appeals case that upheld a ruling rejecting the admissibility of expert testimony

---

[9] The importance of image quality for biometric systems and the need to evaluate image quality across multiple factors jointly rather than a single factor at a time was also noted. To incorporate a measure for image quality, the possibility of tagging the quality was suggested to account for quality differences (difference in granularity, in lighting, in aging, and so on).

[10] As a point of clarification and context, it was noted that before evidence can be put before a jury or, in theory, a court, there may need to be a number of preliminary determinations. Such determinations may include whether the evidence is excludable as hearsay or whether it is relevant, scientific, and sufficiently reliable. Additionally, the debate about admissibility takes place in front of the judge rather than the jury. There may be experts on both sides, and federal judges may appoint their own experts. However, these rules apply only to evidence presented to juries and not to warrant requests.

about a then-new technique that could identify the act of lying by measuring systolic blood pressure.[11] The decision recognized, however, that courts *would* permit expert testimony derived from "a well-recognized scientific principle or discovery, when it is sufficiently established to have gained general acceptance in the particular field in which it belongs."[12] Over the years, the Frye standard became the dominant criterion for admitting scientific evidence. Under Frye, a court would decide if general acceptance had been shown by looking to expert testimony and the existence of publications, by determining that the scientific technique had been put to nonjudicial uses, and by considering other cases that might manifest judicial acceptance.

The second standard, "scientific validity," emerged in *Daubert v. Merrell Dow Pharmaceuticals*, a case that involved birth defects from an antinausea drug known as Bendectin.[13] In this ruling, the Supreme Court overturned the decision of the lower courts to exclude evidence of toxicological epidemiology on the grounds that there was not general acceptance. Given the difficulty of determining when general acceptance has been reached, the Court deemed the Frye test to be inappropriate, under the Federal Rules of Evidence, for governing admissibility, and determined that the evidence admitted should constitute "scientific knowledge" and "be supported by appropriate validation."[14] The general guidance offered for the admissibility of evidence obtained by new scientific techniques included the following considerations: whether the theory or technique has been or could be tested, with appropriate controlling standards in applying the test; whether it has been subjected to peer review and publication; whether the potential rate of error is known; and, more broadly, whether the theory or technique is generally accepted.[15]

As an example, in applying these standards to mitochondrial DNA evidence obtainable from a strand of hair, it was noted that this type of evidence has been admissible in courts even in the case of comparatively small or unrepresentative sample sets. In a mitochondrial DNA match, the proposition that it is "almost always" maternally inherited and "usually" remains constant over time is generally accepted. Mitochondrial DNA has also been accurately sequenced in a laboratory, and the frequency of mitochondrial haplotypes can be estimated to determine if two samples being analyzed are similar.[16]

It was noted that questions pertaining to the theory and appropriateness of the computer algorithms used to perform facial recognition, a relatively new type of biometric identification, would need to be answered to determine the technique's admissibility in a court of law. It would be important to know if the algorithm has been adequately tested and the results have been published or if it is proprietary and not published; whether there is sufficient research literature demonstrating the validity of the approach; whether conditional error probabilities have been established and, if so, their values; and how the matches are presented (e.g., in a binary form or as the probability that the two signals come from a common source); and, finally, whether it is generally accepted that the algorithm makes correct identifications.

---

[11] This technique has been described as a precursor to the polygraph test.

[12] *Frye v. United States*, 293 F. 1013 (C.A.D.C 1923). The Frye opinion is available online at <http://www.daubertontheweb.com/frye_opinion.htm>.

[13] *Daubert v. Merrell Dow Pharmaceuticals, Inc.*, 509 U.S. 579 (1993).

[14] The Daubert decision is not binding on the states, but more than half the states have adopted the Daubert standard to determine the admissibility of evidence in state courts.

[15] These factors, from a nonexclusive list by Justice Blackmun in *Daubert v. Merrell Dow Pharmaceuticals, Inc.*, have become known as the Daubert factors.

[16] An example of the use of DNA evidence in the Scott Peterson case was provided. An FBI analyst testified that a hair found in Scott Peterson's boat could not have been his, and that it matched Lacey Peterson's mother's mitochondrial DNA that should have been inherited by Lacey, the victim. Furthermore, the analyst testified that this haplotype would be seen in one out of 112 Caucasians, based on an FBI database of several thousand. It was noted that this type of evidence is generally admissible despite the statistically unrepresentative sample population of the database.

With regard to latent fingerprints, the form of biometric identification evidence with the longest use, courts historically have accepted this type of evidence under the Frye standard, and it continues to be accepted. However, the application of analysis, comparison, evaluation, and verification (ACE-V), performed by fingerprint analysts, has recently been challenged under the Daubert standard. The problem surrounding fingerprints lies with ACE-V and the human analysis, which some claim lacks scientific rigor—with respect, for instance, to establishing the known error rates and in the controlling standards used by the examiners. As a result, this identification technique continues to be subject to scrutiny; whether court challenges to it will succeed is an open question.[17]

It was noted that defense attorneys try to subpoena basic biometric methods information in an attempt to prevent biometric identification data from being introduced in courts; if it is introduced, they try to identify a factor that will compromise the accuracy and/or validity of the biometric method used. In the discussion, it was suggested that a defense based on the Daubert standard is generally a last resort but can be important when fingerprint evidence is critical to the case.

Lessons for Biometric System Security from the Use of Social Security Numbers

Lessons learned from the use and treatment of SSNs and the related problem of identity fraud were applied to understand and strengthen the security of biometric systems. One problem with the expanded use of SSNs in combination with publicly available personal information (e.g., mother's maiden name) as an identifier, or "key," to gain access to an individual's credit records and other authoritative credentials is their lack of secrecy, given the ease with which they can be shared, sold, and compromised.[18] In the computer science world, it was noted, keys or passwords are kept secret to prevent access to the system by an unauthorized user.[19] While keeping information secret may be a common practice for online and other remote applications, it is common as well in the process of establishing credentials in the physical world, where fake identities can be created by using SSNs and other personal information that is presumed secret or private to acquire so-called "breeder" documents (e.g., driver's licenses) that can be used to gain access to an individual's personal or financial information.

To prevent similar problems with new biometric identifiers and the loss of the "keys" that breed fraud, a law was proposed at the workshop that would prohibit the selling or sharing of unencrypted biometric data. Similar to recently proposed legislation to prohibit the "sale or display of social security numbers,"[20] the draft law aims to minimize access to high-quality images of biometrics (irises, fingerprints, and so on) to keep the new keys more secure, particularly for their use in legal identification. Such a law would shift onto those who would sell or display biometric identifiers the burden of explaining why that sale or display should be warranted. Among the several biometrics that are excluded by the rule are photographs of faces, which have many nonsecurity uses

---

[17] The lengthiest Daubert hearing on fingerprints that was recently affirmed was *U.S. v. Byron Mitchell*, Criminal Action No. 96-407, U.S. District Court for the Eastern District of Pennsylvania, July 1999.

[18] The personal and financial information for 145,000 people that was recently lost by ChoicePoint was provided as an example of compromised data, as key information that can be used to gain access to an individual's financial information becomes accessible to others.

[19] For more on this approach, see Peter Swire, 2004, "A model for when disclosure helps security: What is different about computer and network security?" Journal on Telecommunications and High Technology Law, Vol. 2. Available online at <http://ssrn.com/abstract=531782>.

[20] In an effort to prevent identity theft, the Social Security Number Misuse Prevention Act (S. 29), introduced by Senators Feinstein and Leahy in January 2005, aims to prohibit, among other actions, the sale or display of SSNs to the public without the individual's consent. For more information, see also Mark Roy, 2005, "Feinstein tightens ID theft proposal." Internetnews.com, April 12. Available online at <http://www.internetnews.com/security/article.php/3497161>.

and are generally not secret, as well as DNA used for medical treatment and research. Additionally, it was suggested that encryption should be encouraged as a best practice in the transmission and storage of biometric identifiers. The recent loss of unencrypted backup tapes storing financial and credit card purchase data for 1.2 million federal employees and U.S. senators by the Bank of America was cited to illustrate the need for such practices.[21] Without encryption, a database of biometric identifiers is as vulnerable to unauthorized release as other kinds of personal data. Notwithstanding the challenges in acquiring a new SSN, it is certainly more difficult to replace a compromised fingerprint, for instance, than an SSN. It was argued that without such a law and without encryption, biometric approaches to security, particularly their use as presumably private keys, could fail just as applications using SSNs for secure authentication have failed already.

During the discussion, several questions were raised about the proposed biometric legislation, including how to distinguish which biometrics are worthy of protection and how they could be defined. For instance, it was noted that it may be possible to obtain iris information from a high-resolution photograph. However, there was some agreement by the participants that even though biometrics such as fingerprints are not secret and can be obtained by anyone determined to collect them, it may be useful to restrict the release of fingerprint information online. It was noted that a fingerprint that can be collected from a surface may not have adequate detail to be used in an attack on a system. It was also suggested that such a practice would keep the cost of attack high, as obtaining fingerprints individually is much more expensive than obtaining them in a fingerprint database.

Legal and Societal Issues of Biometric Technologies

To assess what "privacy" means in relation to the use of biometrics technologies, a few on-going research efforts were discussed, beginning with an overview of the legal doctrine and normative expectations of privacy and its potential applicability to biometrics technology and followed by a brief presentation of preliminary findings of some early survey research designed to elicit public opinion about privacy concerns related to the use of biometrics technology.[22] A distinction was made between the factual parameters of privacy—constitutional, statutory, and common law protections—and the normative perceptions of privacy. It was suggested that although factual legal doctrine does not directly relate to biometric technology, principles from constitutional cases defining protections against searches and seizures and in the realms of informational privacy and intimate decision making were applicable for the development of biometric technology policy. Furthermore, normative expectations of privacy also must be taken into consideration and might well be decisive for the acceptance of the broader use of biometric technologies.

It was noted that although the constitutional doctrine of informational privacy is not fully developed, it provides general guidance for the balance that should be struck between the use of biometric identifiers to enhance security and/or to increase convenience and the individual right to privacy. In *Whalen v. Roe* (1973), a foundational case, the Supreme Court was asked to consider if the accumulation of statistical information as part of the "war on drugs" encroached on a reasonable expectation of privacy regarding an individual's arrest and drug rehabilitation records. The Court ruled that in such situations an individual's interest in informational privacy always has to be weighed against the societal objective. It was suggested that this constitutional case provides some principles

---

[21] See Paul Shread, 2005, "Bank's tape loss puts spotlight on backup practices," Internetnews.com, February 28. Available online at <http://www.internetnews.com/storage/article.php/3486036>.

[22] Part of a larger project being funded by the National Science Foundation and the Department of Homeland Security to explore obstacles to the maturity of biometric technology, this research aims to provide a sociolegal assessment through the use of various surveys that would gauge the public's privacy concerns and social perceptions of biometric technology.

to consider, particularly in terms of the interest in storing and sharing biometrics information and the need to also protect privacy.

It was suggested that several cases within the realm of intimate decision making, though only tangentially related, may indicate some potential concerns about and barriers to the collection of biometric information. *Griswold v. Connecticut* (1965) established a realm of intimate decision making around contraceptive usage. In a more recent federal case, *Planned Parenthood Federation of America v. Ashcroft* (2004), the Court was asked to consider whether or not individual privacy rights precluded the Justice Department from gathering information on how many abortions had been performed at a particular clinic. The Court found that the privacy rights in that information were a barrier, and it prohibited the gathering of the statistical information because it intruded on the intimate decision making of the individuals served by the clinic. It was suggested that principles illustrated by this case might inform the limits to using biometric identifiers to access information on the intimate decision making processes of individuals.

In addition to the overview of the legal doctrine of privacy, the initial results from a limited 100-person survey on privacy were discussed, and the designs of proposed surveys following on the initial survey were described.[23] The preliminary results from the small survey sample as described to workshop participants include the following:

- Privacy was by far the greatest concern among the various concerns expressed.
- Concerns about technological fallibilities and procedures to rectify technological failures were also raised.
- Acceptance of biometric technology will increase as technology reliability improves.
- Two of the lesser concerns were inappropriate information sharing, in either government or private sector settings, and the theft of biometric identifiers. The low ranking of these concerns was a surprising survey result.
- Perceptions of biometric technology varied depending on the context of use. For instance, inconvenience was a concern with the use of biometric identifiers at automated teller machines (ATMs) or banks, but there was general support for biometric identifiers when boarding an airplane.

A preliminary suggestion from the survey data was that the public may generally accept the need for give-and-take between expectations of privacy and societal objectives. The public seemed willing to weigh privacy concerns against the purpose of biometrics usage. Relative to this finding, the importance of contextualizing the use of biometrics was also stressed so that polices could be constructed to address different privacy concerns.

During the discussion, a participant suggested that legislation intended to control the use of biometrics technology and protect privacy through the creation of consent provisions is not a panacea, as it would not sufficiently address other issues, such as technological and administrative safeguards and information-sharing rules, that might arise with the use of biometrics technology and that are often not well understood by the public. It was suggested that a broader policy perspective would help to address related issues that will have impacts on privacy. Such concerns were echoed by other

---

[23] The proposed research surveys that will be conducted include (1) a 2,000-person end user survey of those who have been exposed to biometric technology, to understand users' perceptions and acceptance of biometric technology after having been exposed to it as well as existing concerns and problems with the technology; (2) a 1,000-person national random digit dialing survey to compare the perceptions of biometric users with those of nonusers; and (3) a 2,000-person international end user survey to explore and compare different societal notions of privacy, needed since biometrics technologies such as those that are part of US-VISIT (see summary of Session 5) will increasingly involve cross-jurisdictional issues.

participants, who suggested that privacy issues and fair information practices should be proactively addressed rather than relying on the courts, which may not be effective in developing coherent policy.

Issues Related to Policies on Biometrics Data Collection and Use in the Workplace

Several issues emerging from a study recently conducted on RFID tags in the workplace[24] were discussed and related to those that might arise with the use of biometric technologies. The study gathered data from six large private corporations in the United States that required employees to swipe access cards embedded with an RFID chip to gain access to buildings. Four findings from the study were these:

- The data generated by the access cards were sometimes used for much more than controlling building access, including for monitoring adherence to workplace norms and rules, investigating inappropriate activities such as asset thefts, and accessing medical health information in emergencies.
- Appropriate uses of data tended to be determined by security units rather than by executive management, without policies or guidelines for data sharing having been established.
- Data in all surveyed organizations were kept indefinitely, with no retention schedule, and were never independently audited.
- Employees using the swipe cards had not been informed about data retention and alternative data uses.

It was noted that the study—given that it explores issues related to access control and identification, and given that there are proposed applications that would combine biometrics and RFID tags—raised concerns about the use of biometric technologies in the workplace, including these:

- Were the practices seen in the gathering and use of RFID data likely to be precedents for similar practices with data generated by biometric technologies, or will explicit policies be developed comparable to policies for computers, networks, and e-mail?
- Because individuals may not be cognizant of the collection of biometric data, especially for remote-sensing applications, how should, or could, they be notified, and how could their consent be solicited?
- As biometric data will probably be linked to other databases, either directly or through association with an RFID code, identifying individuals by matching newly collected data sets against extant data sets will become more feasible. How will concerns about this new capability be addressed? How long should the collected data be retained?[25]
- Will individuals be given the opportunity to inspect and to correct biometric information collected about them? How will this be done?

---

[24] Edward Balkovich, Tora K. Bikson, and Gordon Bitko, 2005, "9 to 5: Do you know if your boss knows where you are? Case studies of radio frequency identification usage in the workplace," Research brief and report available online at <http://www.rand.org/publications/RB/RB9107/>.

[25] Several models include the OECD Guidelines on the Protection of Privacy and Transborder Flows of Personal Data, available online at http://www.oecd.org/document/18/0,2340,en_2649_34255_1815186_1_1_1_1,00.html, and the European Union privacy directive, which limits retention to a period appropriate to the purpose for which the data were collected (more information can be found at <http://www.epic.org/privacy/intl/data_retention.html>).

- Who should be entitled to access the collected data, and what will be this entity's responsibilities for data integrity, protection, and notification?

International Perspectives

Participants also raised several international legal and normative concerns that have implications for the use of biometrics. Different privacy and data collection laws and regulations may have an impact on what technological capabilities will be permitted. Often, cultural and legal differences can affect monitoring rules in the workplace. While it is commonly understood in the United States that the employer runs the computer system and can monitor the network for security purposes, employees in France and Germany have the right to confidential communications while they are sitting at their office desks, and employers are required to obtain a wiretap to read an employee's e-mails that go through the employer's system. This could present difficulties, particularly for a global company that is trying to implement standard procedures across the organization. In addition, there is a broader view of personal information under European law, which uses the term "identifiable" rather than the more narrowly conceived term "personally identified information" under American law—the former suggesting that the connection between the information and the person is determinable even if no explicit connection is immediately accessible.

During the discussion, a participant alluded to the current attempt of the International Organization for Standardization/International Electrotelecommunications Commission (ISO/IEC's) Joint Technical Committee 1 Standards Committee 37 to develop voluntary best practices for the international use of biometric technology in private corporations by 2006. The international working group aims to bring together different cultural and legal perspectives into a common framework of principles based on fair information practices. The effort is intended to help companies recognize the importance of keeping their workforces informed about the use and implications of biometric technologies.

SESSION 4: SCENARIOS AND APPLICATIONS

Panelists: Joseph Atick, Rick Lazarick, Tony Mansfield, Cynthia Musselman, and Marek Rejman-Greene
Moderator: Gordon Levin

Session 4 participants were asked to discuss the impact of different application contexts on the performance of biometric systems and to describe the general characteristics of successfully deployed biometric systems. Other topics covered in this session included approaches to the fusion of multiple biometric techniques and methods for integrating biometrics into particular systems and environments. Some of the themes that emerged during the discussion were the following:

- The challenges identified for biometric identity management applications will vary depending on the application requirements, system scale, and the security environment.
- Nontechnical factors such as human factors and user training can have significant impacts on biometric system performance.
- Standards and interoperability are important for better system performance and the global use of biometric systems.

Identity, Identity Management, and Biometrics

For identity management applications, one panelist referred to biometrics as the glue that can bind four elements: authorized actions, trust, reputation, and identity.[26] In the identity management process being described, the decision to authorize an action, from logging into a network to entering a country, is operationally based on a level of trust that relies on an individual's reputation, which is linked to an identity. By matching an individual's live biometric against the enrolled or reference sample of that individual, the system can associate actions with an identity based on levels of trust and reputation established for the individual.[27] "Risky" identities can also be flagged by comparing the biometric in question to biometrics in other databases to determine, for example, if an individual's biometric matches that of someone who has been placed on a watch list.

Though biometrics can be used to link these four elements, the panelists stressed that establishing a human identity involves more than capturing a biometric. An individual's identity can be established initially in a number of ways, depending on the application needs and context. For instance, the identity can be linked to a unique enrollment that tracks information from day one forward but does not reveal the individual's legal name (the approach used by eBay, albeit not with biometrics). Alternatively, a legal identity can be established by linking historical and document-based information such as that contained on a driver's license or passport. One account was given of a remote village chief vouching for an individual's proper name when no paper documents existed.

An underlying problem with large-scale biometric identity management applications that rely on paper-based documents to establish a legal identity lies not so much in capturing the biometrics, it was suggested, but in creating and trusting the linkages.[28] A panelist called the mapping of a traditional, paper-based identity to a biometrics-based identity the Achilles' heel of biometric identity management applications. This mapping process creates an opportunity for identity laundering (the legitimizing of a "bad" identity) when documents can be falsified and used to bypass the reputation discovery processes to obtain a "clean" identity. A panelist also noted that tying a biometrics-based identity to multiple paper-based documents is a time-intensive process that would require traditional investigations to determine if the documents are authentic. In discussion this problem was illustrated by national ID card applications, which would presumably entail a gradual linking of an initial ID to more assets and information (e.g., mortgage and credit history) after initial establishment of the linkage between an individual and his/her national ID. However, national ID cards would probably not adequately deter identity theft or identity laundering, presumably an intended purpose of such an application. In addition to the challenges of linking identity information to a biometric, it was suggested that other applications—such as an e-passport intended for the global recognition or assignment of a legal identity for an individual—would require open interoperability standards to enable the exchange of information across governments. Such cards would likely require the creation of a federated identity system, or silos of identity, rather than a single, centralized identity.[29]

---

[26] There was not time for in-depth discussions of the meanings of these terms and their interrelationship at the workshop.

[27] Dynamic knowledge discovery was also briefly touched on as a mechanism to reassess and update an individual's reputation (based, for example, on periodic reinvestigations vs. a one-time investigation) in order to adjust levels of trust used to authorize or revoke access rights on a timely basis.

[28] One participant cautioned that the biometrics themselves, used to create and fix the linkages to identity, are not secret.

[29] A previous NRC report explored the question of a nationwide identity system at length: see S. Kent and L. Millett, eds., IDs—Not That Easy: Questions About Nationwide Identity Systems. National Research Council. Washington, D.C., 2002.

Application Contexts and Security Environments

Panelists discussed some of the characteristics of and challenges for biometrics systems in relation to different application contexts (e.g., large versus small deployments) and security environments (in the case discussed, government versus commercial). Some of the challenges particular to a large-scale, government (rather than commercial) biometric identification application were discussed, and some solutions were presented.

The national ID card[30] being developed by the United Kingdom was described. The central challenge identified at the workshop was the need to establish realistic policy and performance requirements for the biometric technologies in light of the system scale and the diverse enrollment population. The system scale of 60 million users introduces significant challenges for achieving the required performance metrics (a false nonmatch rate of less than 1 percent, or 1 in 100, and a false match rate of less than 0.1 percent, or 1 in 1,000), as these rates are not directly measurable without an operational system or a large database for testing. The system scale and related costs of enrollment also raise questions about the age requirement for initial enrollment and the frequency of re-enrollment in the system. A second distinct and critical requirement for a national biometric system is the need for universal enrollment across all sectors of society. It is not known if biometrics can be inclusive of all sectors, as few tests have been conducted that represent society as a whole. However, it is known that a small fraction of the population will not be capable of providing an adequate sample, as a consequence of inherited biology or temporary or permanent conditions—for example, fingerprint damage in the form of a cut, burn, or scarring; arthritic fingers for hand geometry, and some eye injuries or conditions for iris recognition. Furthermore, a policy requirement for a mandatory and universally deployed national system in the United Kingdom is that it must be nondiscriminatory, both in perception and in actuality, to individuals with disabilities or specific cultural or ethnic backgrounds. The system must also accommodate those who are not familiar with the biometric technology and process as well as those who intend to be uncooperative.

The potential solutions offered by the panelists for the false nonmatch rate and enrollment problems include the improvement of sensors and system ergonomics in order to acquire higher quality biometrics. To further minimize enrollment problems, it was suggested that users be permitted to choose a second biometric modality for enrollment. If multibiometric fusion is involved, multi-instance rather than multimodal fusion would simplify user training.

Panelists drew clear distinctions between the purposes and functions of commercial vs. government biometric applications. Commercial applications aim to provide convenience and assistance to voluntary users in targeted sectors. Two possible applications are the personalization of services and the facilitation of individual accountability; in the latter, an individual's name, reputation, and biometric accompany a transaction to allow for tracking over time. To be operationally viable, commercial applications must be able to tolerate some error in enrollment rates among the user population.[31] Additionally, performance should degrade gracefully, and operations should include redundancy. Some hypothesize that to achieve widespread acceptance among a voluntary user population, the technology should facilitate clever, personally useful applications that are reasonably routine, transparent, and, as one participant called for, "cool." The use of the technology should be intuitive, and its purpose should be clear and understandable to the user. The

---

[30] The national ID card aims to reduce the registration of multiple identities and establish a single, verifiable identity per individual that will be linked to a previously established (document-based) identity and used for national identification purposes when an individual appears to receive government services.

[31] A panelist noted that in some cases an extra measure of security (performance) might not be worth the reduction in throughput. It was suggested that rather than always striving for 100 percent accuracy, the target error rate should depend on the type of application: In other words, it should be "good enough" for the application.

example given—an integrated mobile device, a hypothetical commercial application combining the functionality of a mobile phone and a personal data assistant—illustrated some of these characteristics. It could be an individual's primary device for communication and information access, and the biometric could be used to provide secure access. Other information could be used by the system, including a personal identification number, an equipment-unique identifier, physical location, other biometrics (voice, face, fingerprint), and history of use.

It was suggested that user-centered design principles be applied to develop application features and to determine the features' value and usefulness. Recent findings suggest that the utility and convenience of biometrics may somewhat lessen privacy concerns as individual users begin to explore and weigh the costs and benefits.[32]

Nontechnical Factors and General System Characteristics

Panelists identified additional nontechnological factors that impact the performance of biometric systems:

- The type of biometric system will impact user behavior and system performance. For instance, in a system that aims to verify a claim of enrollment, such as in the administration of government benefits, the individual is trying to produce a matching result. By contrast, in a system that aims to verify a claim (sometimes implicit) of nonenrollment, such as screening for inclusion on a watch list, the individual is trying to avoid a match.[33]
- Human factors are critical for optimizing the capture performance of biometric techniques. Attention to system ergonomics that automatically adapt to human factors, such as a facial recognition camera that adjusts to differences in height and presentation, can make a system less intimidating and more natural for users and may significantly reduce enrollment error rates. It was suggested that systems that provide useful feedback to users and systems that incorporate touch screen technology rather than a keyboard enhance capture and enrollment performance.
- Training is useful for system operators to understand system operations but should not be needed for users as the systems should be sufficiently intuitive. Some panelists noted that training did improve sample collection in deployed systems; others stressed that user training could have the opposite effect because it could teach a user who chooses to be noncompliant how to improperly enroll.

Participants noted that successfully deployed biometric applications tend to have the following characteristics:

- The ability to select out individuals who cannot provide or have difficulty providing a good quality sample for a given modality.
- Robustness to variation in the false rejection rate, given that some error is to be expected with a biometric system.

---

[32] Findings from BIOVISION, a project sponsored by the European Commission to explore successful biometric deployments from a user and system integrator perspective.

[33] Adversarial analysis is a hard problem to solve because real numbers for false reject and accept rates are difficult to obtain from adversaries who have successfully defeated a system. In addition, an adversary may purposely inflict an injury to create a legitimate problem of entering through a biometric system, requiring a secondary entry procedure.

- Realistic system performance requirements with respect to the application and the technology, offering an effective improvement for the particular application at a reasonable cost.

Standards and Global Interoperability of Biometric Systems

To illustrate the importance of standards setting and the interoperability of systems, panelists highlighted early work in multibiometric standards formation and data collection as well as the results from a recent interoperability test. For future integration of multibiometric systems, ISO/IEC's Joint Technical Committee 1 Standards Committee 37[34] has focused on defining multibiometric terminology to develop standardized approaches for assessing and improving multibiometric fusion.[35] The terminology development process provided the background to break down the problem (see Box 2.4).

It was suggested that if designed and implemented effectively, multibiometric approaches have the potential to improve biometric system performance—that is, to reduce the false acceptance rate (FAR), the false rejection rate (FRR), the failure to enroll (FTE) rate, and the failure to acquire (FTA) rate—and can be more resistant to spoofing.

However, participants noted that one challenge to research in multibiometric fusion techniques has been the limited supply of true multibiometric data (i.e., multibiometric data from the same human being). Typical studies have involved tens to several hundreds of individuals. In attempts to achieve large multibiometric data sets, some researchers have assumed that biometric samples from completely different modalities (e.g., face, fingerprint, iris) are fully uncorrelated. Based on this assumption, they may create a chimeric multibiometric data sample by combining a facial image from one individual, a fingerprint from another individual, and an iris image from another individual. To validate this assumption and evaluate multibiometric systems, NIST and TSA, at the time of the workshop, were planning a 2005 deployment of the Multimodal Biometric Accuracy Research Kiosk (MBARK) to collect face, fingerprint, and iris data from the same individuals. The importance of independent testing was discussed, along with the remaining work to be done in the development of worldwide applications that will rely on biometric technology. A third-party test to evaluate the compliance of several commercial technologies with a secondary standard modeled after the draft ISO standard revealed poor performance and interoperability among the vendors that were tested. The test, conducted on seven different products and using biometric data gathered from volunteers from the intended user population,[36] had three components: (1) conformance to the requirements of the standard; (2) performance of the system, consisting of a sensor and an algorithm each from different providers; and (3) the interoperability of the systems. When multiple sensors were tested against one algorithm, there were large (up to 40 percent) differences in performance among the biometric systems. Within the small test sample, only two sets of product combinations (each consisting of a distinct sensor and an algorithm) were interoperable

---

[34] The technical report *Multi-modal and Other Multi-biometric Fusion* was issued by Working Group 2 of ISO/IEC JTC1 SC37 with support and technical contributions from the International Committee for Information Technology Standards (INCITS) M1 Technical Committee on Biometrics—Ad Hoc Group on Evaluating Multi-biometric Systems (AHGEMS).

[35] Fusion has been implemented for many years in large automated fingerprint identification systems (AFISs) using multi-instance and multialgorithmic approaches.

[36] The test sample of 125 was smaller than the anticipated 225 participants. Though it did not include any noncooperative users, it was drawn from the user population and was representative of some of the problems users of biometrics systems may confront.

and achieved the target FAR and FRR of 1 percent out of the 125 participants.[37] Despite the few technologies that passed this independent evaluation, to be accepted in this arena, all future products must meet or exceed the performance and interoperability levels that have already been set.

BOX 2.4
Multibiometric Systems

Multibiometric systems comprise four distinct subcategories—multimodalities (e.g., finger, iris, face), multi-instances (e.g., right and left index fingers or multiple images of a face or scene), multisensors (e.g., optical, capacitive, and ultrasonic), and/or multialgorithms (different matchers)—that can be fused at four different levels: the decision level, the score level, the signal level, and the feature level. At the feature level, the biometric samples can be combined to create a feature space for processing in the matching (score) and decision levels. Current fusion approaches occur at the score level, where scores assigned by each biometric channel are combined before the system issues a decision based on the score. To enhance score fusion, prior probabilities that approximate prior beliefs of experts can be taken into account and score normalization between matching algorithms can also be used to provide additional information when implementing a fusion scheme. Other fusion approaches that can be systematically applied to improve fusion accuracy and/or throughput include combination techniques such as summing rules and products or combining different classifiers, the use of layering or cascading logic when gathering and using multiple measures and sources of information, and simultaneous versus sequential sample presentation while capturing information.

SESSION 5: TECHNICAL AND POLICY ASPECTS OF INFORMATION SHARING AND COOPERATION

Panelists: William Casey, Patty Cogswell, Neal Latta, K.A. Taipale, and John Woodward
Moderator: Peter Higgins

In Session 5, panelists were asked to discuss a variety of issues related to biometric data sharing, including technical challenges as they relate to synchronicity and connectivity of data on the one hand and security and privacy of data on the other hand; policy considerations for sharing biometric data between agencies; and practical consideration of standards development and cross-jurisdictional cooperation. The following are some of the topics covered in this session:

- Newly established and long-standing biometric data-sharing applications at the state, national, and international levels were described in the contexts of military defense, law enforcement, and immigration. Systems discussed included the Automated Biometric Identification System (ABIS), the Criminal Alien Identification System (CAIS), the Integrated Automated Fingerprint Identification System (IAFIS), and the United States Visitor and Immigrant Status Indicator Technology (US-VISIT) program.

---

[37] The test involved one-to-one verification between a seafarer's biometric and the two fingerprints stored on the ID card. A false accept scenario consisted of stealing the issued IDs and being a close enough match to another seafarer's stored biometric. Problems posed by larger databases, such as the legitimacy of issued IDs and other matching problems, were not part of the test. For more information, see International Labour Organization, 2004, Seafarers Identity Documents Convention (Revised), 2003 (No. 185), ILO Seafarers' Identity Documents, Biometric Testing Campaign Report. Part I. Geneva. Available online at <http://www.ilo.org/public/english/dialogue/sector/sectors/mariti/sid.pdf>.

- Technical and policy challenges related to information sharing among large-scale biometrics systems were addressed, including data integrity and procedural analysis, consolidation of biometric information, and integration of databases.
- Broader policy challenges of biometric information sharing also were discussed, including (1) the importance of evaluating biometric systems based on their context, purpose, and the policies they serve; (2) establishing criteria to determine the usefulness of data for decision making; and (3) instituting careful procedures for maintaining and sharing digital records.

Automated Biometric Identification System

The Automated Biometric Identification System (ABIS), a new biometric identification system designed by the Department of Defense (DOD), was described as a system modeled after the FBI's Integrated Automated Fingerprint Identification System (IAFIS) (see Box 2.5) for the collection, storage, and sharing of overseas biometric data within the military and with other government organizations for counterterrorism purposes. A guiding concept for the system was described as "identity dominance," or the use of biometrics to increase the level of confidence in the linkages between individuals and their previous identities, criminal histories, or terrorist activities in the United States and in other countries.[38]

The conceptual architecture of ABIS, similar to the information architecture of IAFIS, aims to integrate into one database information (in electronically searchable format) from operations and other sources that has been gathered by combatant commands (COCOMs). The collected biometric data would include 10 rolled fingerprints, mug shots, and a DNA sample. The DNA sample, it was noted, would be handled separately; fingerprints and mug shots would be stored in ABIS and searched against the ABIS database for possible matches. The fingerprints also would be shared with the FBI, according to information-sharing policies, and searched against the FBI's IAFIS database to identify any matches with existing U.S. criminal records.

ABIS was described as a type of "biometric-based identity management service provider" in the situation where DOD determines if any samples match and sends those results to other national security organizations on a need-to-know basis. There is also general interest in developing procedures for sharing information with the Department of Homeland Security (DHS). Since becoming operational in the summer of 2004, ABIS has been used to identify individuals in Iraq as former detainees and as individuals with U.S. criminal histories.

Criminal Alien Identification System

As presented by one of the panelists, the Criminal Alien Identification System (CAIS) is a pilot biometric information-sharing system within the Boston Police Department that was developed to recognize foreign-born individuals illegally residing in the United States and to facilitate access to information about immigration violations.[39] The panelist described the process as follows: When an individual is arrested on any charge, 10 rolled fingerprints, mug shots, and information on distinguishing features such as tattoos are entered and stored in CAIS. The same information is entered in the Massachusetts State Police Department's Automated Fingerprint Identification System (AFIS), the FBI's IAFIS (see Box 2.5), and, if necessary, shared with Immigration and Customs

---

[38] Identity dominance is analogous in some ways to the concept of identity management discussed in Session 1.

[39] Based on a study conducted by the Boston Police Department, 19 percent of its arrestees had immigration issues of varying seriousness.

Enforcement (ICE).[40] These data are searched against the FBI's IAFIS database, with responses generally returning in 15 to 20 minutes.[41] If the arrestee was not born in the United States, the information is sent to ICE in Boston, which begins an investigation. For serious crimes, Interpol also has fingerprint search capability across multiple jurisdictions. The panelist also noted that the Boston Police Department audits department practices and issues sanctions for data misuse.

BOX 2.5
Integrated Automated Fingerprint Identification System

As described by several panelists, the FBI's Integrated Automatic Fingerprint Identification System (IAFIS) criminal master file is a criminal law enforcement technical capability with a database consisting of over 48 million electronically searchable sets of fingerprints and corresponding criminal history information on individuals arrested in the United States for a felony or serious misdemeanor charge.[1] The panelists highlighted some of the system capabilities that facilitate the linking of past criminal records across jurisdictions and contribute to a high degree of accuracy and effectiveness in biometric identification. IAFIS became operational in July 1999.

The panelists described the information entered into IAFIS during the criminal booking process as including 10 rolled fingerprints and a mug shot. They noted that the FBI receives around 25,000 criminal fingerprint submissions per day from law enforcement at the local, state, and federal level and around 25,000 civil requests from DHS, the Office of Personnel Management, school boards, etc. that are searched against IAFIS to determine if the individual has been involved in any previous criminal activities.[2] Unlike the criminal transactions, the majority of the civil search transactions are not entered into the IAFIS repository. As most information that is entered into the databases, including criminal bookings, investigations, and other operations and information[3] comes from state and local police departments,[4] the panelists emphasized the importance of the advisory policy process conducted by the FBI's Criminal Justice Information Services (CJIS). The advisory policy board—consisting of local and state representatives—serves to advise the FBI on data management issues and has worked to develop standards, perform audits of state repositories, and issue sanctions for misuses of data.

---

[1] In addition to storing criminal fingerprints in IAFIS, the panelists noted that military fingerprints are also stored in the database but are not searched routinely in criminal cases. Federal employees' and police officers' fingerprints also are enrolled in the database, but not all are in electronic form. Furthermore, IAFIS contains fingerprints for both living and deceased individuals (albeit with conservative criteria by which a set of prints may be marked as belonging to a deceased individual).

[2] Law enforcement studies have found that 62 percent of arrestees have a previous criminal history.

[3] The FBI is the repository of U.S. criminal data, including fingerprints, the Interstate Identification Index, national files for warrants, sex offenders, etc.

[4] The Boston Police Department was the first agency to send fingerprints electronically to the FBI in 1995, an early implementation of an IAFIS function.

---

[40] The information is also shared with the Commonwealth of Massachusetts Probation Department and the Suffolk County District Attorney.

[41] The panelist indicated that since 2002, 62,000 arrests had been processed, including 8,153 flagged individuals. Among these were 43 with illegal reentries, 166 with outstanding warrants for removal, 51 with overstayed visa waivers, 207 in removal proceedings, 19 who had been granted relief or whose proceedings had been terminated, and 377 foreign juveniles.

United States Visitor and Immigrant Status Indicator Technology

As discussed in this session, the US-VISIT program[42] centers on issues of immigration and border management during preentry, entry, status management, and exit procedures. In contrast to criminal law enforcement applications, US-VISIT aims to collect, maintain, and share information, including biometrics information, on foreign nationals to help determine who should be permitted to enter, who should be removed, and who should be provided special protection, such as refugees.[43] One of the largest and busiest deployments,[44] US-VISIT captures and stores a digital photograph and two electronically scanned fingerprints for each entrant.

The panelists noted that a core component of US-VISIT[45] is the Biometric Identification System (IDENT) database of the Department of Homeland Security (DHS). The IDENT database, separate from the IAFIS database, comprises several databases, including the following:

- The US-VISIT enrollment database containing biometric information and allowing verification of an individual's records upon entry and exit.
- A watch list and lookout database with information related to terrorists, wanted criminals, sexual offenders, immigration violators, and international fugitives, among other categories. This database is populated with information from the FBI, state or local authorities, DHS, the Department of State, and Interpol.
- A recidivist database[46] containing information (for example, the number of illegal border crossings) about previous DHS apprehensions that does not qualify for entry into the IAFIS or watch list databases.

---

[42] The Illegal Immigration Reform and Immigrant Responsibility Act (IIRIRA) Section 110 created the US-VISIT program in September 1996. Subsequent legislation expanding the program requirements includes the Data Management Improvement Act (DMIA) of 2000; the Visa Waiver Permanent Program Act in 2000, the USA Patriot Act and the Aviation Transportation Security Act in 2001, and the Enhanced Border Security and Visa Entry Reform Act in 2002. More recently, the Intelligence Reform and Terrorism Prevention Act in December 2004 added the requirement to expedite the addition of a biometric to the entry and exit system.

[43] The panelists indicated that since the beginning of the US-VISIT program in January 2004, there have been 5,342 watch list hits, with a 1 percent error rate, out of more than 4.2 million visa applications. At entry, for travelers who are not entered in the systems, 2,375 watch list hits have resulted from the 18.9 million travelers processed. As for the identity verification of travelers, among those who had been previously enrolled, there have been 11,622 mismatches out of about 4.4 million one-to-one matches. For status management, 175,234 new watch list records have been generated, with 131 hits against entry records, 86 hits against visa records, 165 cases referred to ICE, and 4 arrests. Identity verification at the border has resulted in 11,600 false matches among the 4,369,569 one-to-one matches performed. The number of travelers processed through exit controls via an automated kiosk was 355,967, resulting in 54 watch list hits, with no stops or arrests. IDENT has made seven identifications. The panelists noted that all watch list matches, based on a threshold level set by NIST guidelines, go to secondary processing, where human examiners determine if the match is true, false, or a mismatch.

[44] As of January 2004, US-VISIT was operational at 115 airports and 15 seaports; as of December 2004, coverage included 50 land border ports of entry, with the remaining 115 to be covered by December 2005.

[45] US-VISIT includes the interfacing and integration of over 20 existing systems, including, among others, the Arrival Departure Information System (ADIS), storing traveler arrival and departure information; the Advance Passenger Information System (APIS), containing arrival and departure manifest information; Computer Linked Application Information Management System 3 (CLAIMS 3), holding information on foreign nationals who request benefits; the Student Exchange Visitor Information System (SEVIS), containing information on foreign students in the United States; and the Consular Consolidated Database (CCD), containing information about whether an individual holds a valid visa or has previously applied for a visa.

The US-VISIT process was described as follows: During the preentry phase, information on the visa applicant is captured at an overseas consulate and searched against the IDENT and watch list databases. At the point of entry, an individual is enrolled and a search is performed against only the watch list database. The response time for issuance of a visa at a consulate is, on average, approximately 15 minutes; at the point of entry, responses are returned in approximately 10 seconds.[47] Other potential program capabilities include generating an exit record of visitors[48] based on one-to-one verification and status management and maintaining an accurate record of changes in an individual's residence eligibility (for example, marriage to a U.S. citizen) or ineligibility (for example, an expired visa or other immigration violation). The panelists explained that status management consisted of checking IAFIS records (including the new criminal records, which are updated every 24 hours) and the 1.8-million-entry watch list database against the 14-million-entry US-VISIT database to identify new watch list records and to pursue investigations. Requirements for the future evolution of US-VISIT include biometric comparison and travel document authentication for both U.S.-issued travel documents to permanent residents, such as refugees, and visa-waiver program passports issued by other countries.[49] A privacy protection program for US-VISIT was also discussed that included information use rules and notification requirements, redress policies to request corrections of errors, and privacy impact and privacy risk assessments. There is ongoing work to develop information-sharing models with other governments, such as the Enhancing International Travel Security program, intended to enable governments to validate "good" people, not just to identify the "bad."

Policy Challenges Related to Large-Scale Systems

Technical and policy challenges raised by information sharing among large-scale biometrics systems were also discussed. Such challenges include maintaining data integrity, consolidation of biometric information, and integration of databases. Participants also underscored the importance of clearly defining the purpose of a system before adding new requirements to the existing system.

The panelists indicated that to ensure military and civilian agencies are collecting data to the necessary technical standards would require the development of policy to determine that the data are being collected uniformly and by high-quality, sufficiently-trained staff using proper equipment. Panelists also stressed the need to improve the quality of information transmission to facilitate decision making. However, improvements to the analysis procedure also require other organizations to perform intelligence link analysis[50] quickly, which is often difficult given the different missions of the different agencies. For instance, the US-VISIT program operates under certain efficiency constraints, given the need to manage the flow of travelers quickly. When individuals are held in custody suspected of wrongdoing, such as occurs in law enforcement and military operations, more time may be available to return results. Participants noted that the Defense Science Board is

---

[46] The recidivist database, which began in 1994, is the original biometric foundation of US-VISIT and has grown with the addition of the biometric enrollment database.

[47] Currently, more then 25,000 people a day are biometrically checked as part of the visa process. Since January 2004, there have been more than 4 million visa applications. At entry, approximately 75,000 people a day are run through the US-VISIT system.

[48] The panelists noted that the exit record may also be used for identification against watch lists, but it will not be used to enable enrollment.

[49] One factor that could delay the implementation of these requirements is the current difficultly most visa waiver countries are experiencing to meet the deadline and the inability of the United States to acquire readers for these passports.

[50] Intelligence link analysis refers to the process of associating other pieces of data with the biometric match.

beginning to address improvements in the communication of results from the biometric information captured and stored in different agency databases.

The panelists suggested that the greatest challenges in integrating databases were not only the differences in the number of samples (e.g., prints) collected, the time constraints, and conditions of the facilities[51] but also the different contexts in which the information is collected. For instance, IDENT/US-VISIT is generally used in a context where people have incentives to tell the truth and describe their real identities; IAFIS is not. Additionally, individuals in the US-VISIT database are not usually in IAFIS, because they are not likely to have been charged with a crime in the United States.

As the information that a system collects will depend on its intended use, some participants stressed that it is important to clearly identify the problems that the system intends to address before the collection of biometric information is consolidated across government agencies. For instance, the information DHS collects regarding the entry of a foreigner is not necessarily related to the threat that individual poses to a plane, a separate area in which DHS also collects information. Panelists suggested that existing problems should be defined and the best technology should be selected before missions change or are expanded.

Broader Technical and Policy Challenges Related to Biometric Information-Sharing Systems

In examining the broader goals for and challenges of biometrics systems, the importance of evaluating such systems with respect to their purposes and context was stressed, along with the need for policies to establish appropriate error rate goals or thresholds, facilitate the identification of potential sources of error, and promote a better understanding of what improvements biometric systems offer over existing security, access control, and other systems (see Session 3). Furthermore, it was suggested that the scope of the difficult policy problems that should be addressed extends beyond issues of biometric technology and system accuracy to considerations of the usefulness of the data for decision making and to policies for maintaining and sharing digital records.

There was a discussion on the adequate alignment of policy and technological capabilities. Not only is it economically infeasible from a technology and policy perspective to have an error rate of zero, but also such an error rate requirement would imply that no risk assumptions need be considered in designing policy. As both systems and policies must be designed to accommodate failure, it was suggested that redundancies and error handling procedures should be created for both. Additionally, the interaction between the technology—a tool for a particular purpose—and the system must be considered, because the technology choice may also have policy implications. For instance, when liveliness is being screened for (to ensure that the biometric information being detected comes from a living human being), it may be easier for an attacker to emulate liveliness than to defeat or circumvent nonliveliness detection. Given the tight coupling between the technology selection and policy goals, it was suggested that the explicit biometric technology designations in recent legislation might be too specific for Congress to mandate effectively.

In addition to the potential sources of error previously identified in the workshop (see Session 1), it was suggested that human factors should also be considered in addressing insider threats. By some measures, 70 percent of IT system breaches or compromises are reportedly attributable to insider threats. All systems are subject to both intentional and unintentional errors. Participants discussed the

---

[51] It was noted that military field facilities for capturing biometrics differ significantly from those for law enforcement booking and DHS. Currently, the National Institute of Justice has an initiative to design equipment capable of taking 10 high-quality rolled fingerprints accurately in 10 seconds.

trade-offs between secrecy and security: When is openness necessary (for example, in terms of algorithms or error rates) to achieve a robust system, and when is secrecy a better strategy?[52]

It was emphasized that understanding the intended purpose of a biometric system—be it security, "security theater," or social control—is necessary to properly appraise the system's effectiveness. Security theater (for example, requiring display of a driver's license to enter a building, or removal of shoes before entering an airport boarding area—provides little real security protection but may have social value by allowing people to feel more secure. On the other hand, while improving the document security and issuance processes for driver licenses might be worthwhile, there is a need to clarify the purpose of such measures and to carefully distinguish between measures aimed at increased social control and measures aimed at counterterrorism or national security. For instance, the proposed provision of the Real ID Act that requires states to issue drivers' licenses only against proof of legal U.S. residence may begin to address issues of illegal immigration. However, it also may exclude a significant portion of the population from the driver's license system and from any identification systems based on drivers' licenses, preventing the identification of such individuals after the fact. One consequence of this may be to increase the size of the suspect pool that law enforcement and national security resources must be devoted to.

Several participants emphasized that biometrics may improve identification procedures but are not a panacea. Different types of identification have different characteristics, and determining which type is appropriate will depend on the application. Verification of a claim of enrollment, for instance, stands in contrast to identification of a person without an enrollment claim. The former, verification of an enrollment claim, serves to verify the individual identity, often with the subject retaining control over his or her own information. In the latter, identification without an enrollment claim, additional data are attributed and tied to an individual based on biometric identifiers, with third parties generally controlling data attribution and reputation of the subject.[53]

With respect to limiting identity theft, it was suggested that claim verification, where individuals have an incentive to control their reputation, might be more useful than a system in which biometrics are aggregated in a database and later sold, which would not be much better than current processes that aggregate and sell SSNs. With respect to security screening, when attempting identification absent a claim, there are concerns not only about the accuracy of the biometric identifier but also about the usefulness of data that are linked to an identity and used by the system for decision making.[54] If a watch list is being employed, the integrity and usefulness of the data (and by extension the list itself) will depend on the criteria for inclusion on the watch list, on who has responsibility for different segments of a presumably integrated list, and on policy limits that prevent the inclusion of minor offenses that might dilute the data.[55]

Various issues related to information sharing were identified, including clarifying the role of privacy and the differences between the rules for preemption and counterterrorism and those for due process in criminal prosecutions. Several principles for information sharing and biometric system use were offered, including these:

---

[52] For a recent take on this issue, see Peter Swire, 2004, "A model for when disclosure helps security: What is different about computer and network security?" *Journal on Telecommunications and High Technology Law*, Vol. 2. Available online at <http://ssrn.com/abstract=531782>.

[53] Participants suggested that clear policy rules and mechanisms are needed for managing reputation elements and more general data in systems, for matching systems to needs, and for addressing data issues such as transience (or how long information should be maintained) and error correction.

[54] The panelist suggested that data mining presents the reverse problem, as data are used to try to reveal the legal identity; biometric systems begin with the identity to try to reveal the data.

[55] For an overview of problems that can arise with watch lists see, K.A. Taipale, 2004, "Public safety vs. personal privacy: The case for and against secure flight," presented at the InfoSecurity 2004 conference in New York on December 8. Available online at <http://www.stilwell.org/presentations/CAS-InfoSec2004.pdf>.

- Make clear the purpose of the system and how potential intrusion on rights is balanced with functional requirements.
- Identify alternatives and choose less intrusive means to accomplish the objective once the technology has been selected.
- Ensure the ability to correct errors in the system.
- Design system policies that appropriately consider the consequences of different system errors (for example, the consequence of someone gaining access to an airplane versus the consequence of someone's flawed prosecution and wrongful incarceration).

It was emphasized that the lack of clear policies and rules creates problems, particularly because preemptive counterterrorist actions take place in a context that presumes the innocence of foreign travelers and U.S. citizens.

Several principles were offered for biometric system use. First, do no harm. Understand the system design and features that are necessary for the policy purpose. For instance, do not build systems that center on identification rather than security if the rationale for the system is security. Second, limit the harm. Include only those features that are necessary to support the system purpose and process. Third, be aware of unintended consequences (see Session 3). Consider when transaction records are necessary, when they are not, and when records should expire. Additionally, it was suggested that technical systems should include "policy appliances," or mechanisms that (1) permit an intervention point for human beings to make a decision to control data sharing and (2) provide a technical means for carrying it out, which can be adjusted depending on the particular application, threat level, etc.

Appendixes

A
Workshop Agenda

WORKSHOP ON TECHNICAL, POLICY, AND CULTURAL DIMENSIONS OF BIOMETRIC SYSTEMS

March 15-16, 2005
Washington, D.C

Tuesday, March 15

9:15 a.m.　　　　Welcome: Joe Pato

9:30-noon　　　　*Session 1: Scientific and Technical Challenges for Biometric Technologies and Systems, Including System Integration, Architecture, and Contexts of Use*

　　　　　　　　Moderator: Anil Jain

　　　　　　　　Potential Discussion Topics
- Are there major technological breakthroughs on the horizon regarding new modalities, multimodal biometrics, new recognition algorithms, and/or new decision algorithms? What might emerging sensors, MEMS, and nanotechnology offer to biometric systems?
- Do you think biometrics can reliably solve the identity authentication/identification problem, especially when the user is an adversary?
- What are the challenges regarding signal quality, feature persistence over time, statistical dependence among measurements of features within and across times and method of database indexing? How do these challenges relate to the performance of a biometric system?
- What are the advantages or disadvantages of using biometrics to enhance or replace cryptographic authentication protocols?
- How does the context of use impact systems choice, integration and interoperability options, and effectiveness? How does system architecture influence effectiveness?

- What are the most significant open research questions and hard problems in biometrics, and how should they be prioritized?
- Is the current research infrastructure adequate for the needs of biometrics researchers? What kinds of expertise are required (e.g., biology and statistics)? To what extent should biometrics research be a part of federal IT and security research efforts, and which agencies should emphasize which aspects?

Panelists:
Jean-Christophe Fondeur, SAGEM
James Matey, Sarnoff Labs
Sharath Pankanti, IBM
Jonathon Phillips, National Institute of Standards and Technology
David Scott, Rice University

Noon-1:00 p.m.   Lunch

1:00-3:30   *Session 2: Measurement, Statistics, Testing, and Evaluation*

Moderator: Joe Campbell

Potential Discussion Topics
- How can the quality of biometric data capture be assessed with sensitivity to human rights, accessibility, and due process? How can such assessments be used to improve the operation and performance of a biometric system?
- What do we have to know about biometric features in populations in order to accurately estimate the probability that (1) two individuals will be indistinguishable for a particular feature, (2) an individual who expresses one particular feature will also express another particular feature, (3) a particular combination of features is unique to one specific individual, (4) an individual does not express a particular feature, and (5) an individual's ethnic or family background predicts expression of a particular feature? What kind of studies do we need to conduct to collect this information? How large a population will be required for each of the necessary studies? Are the statistical methods currently used for modeling, representing, and reporting the performance of biometric systems fully appropriate? If not, what analytic technologies are available to improve them?
- Is there a role for standard biometric databases made available for research, testing, and development? What are good strategies for reducing the costs associated with compiling test data for biometrics systems?
- What is the appropriate role of government in biometrics testing outside of a procurement process? Should the government test products and should it test the vulnerabilities of biometric products? If so, are there any classification issues that arise, and what are they? How effective are current government-led testing programs, and is their funding structure appropriate to the task?

- To what extent should vendor-specific (and potentially market-affecting) information be made available together with the results of government/public tests of biometric systems?
- What are reasonable time-frame expectations for the development, testing, and deployment of standards, technologies, and systems, and how should the public and Congress be educated about these expectations? Should biometric deployments be certified in some way, and what might that mean?

Panelists:
George Doddington, National Institute of Standards and Technology
Michele Freadman, Massport
Patrick Grother, National Institute of Standards and Technology
Austin Hicklin, Mitretek Systems
Nell Sedransk, National Institute of Standards and Technology

3:30 Break

3:45-6:15 *Session 3: Legislative, Policy, Human, and Cultural Factors*

Moderator: Jeanette Blomberg

Potential Discussion Topics
- What usability, interface, social, and human factors issues arise with the deployment of biometrics systems, and how might they be addressed? How can these factors be used to inform system and interface design?
- How can or should cultural factors be taken into account when designing and deploying biometrics systems?
- What have been the effects of legislative changes that necessitate the increased use of biometric technologies? What new legal issues might be raised by more widespread use?
- What recent policies have shaped the current and near-term use of biometrics technology deployments? What are the policies' desired and actual effects?
- What privacy and autonomy concerns does the increased use of biometrics technologies raise? What are the implications and how can they be addressed? What is the relationship between bodily integrity (personal space) and information privacy concerns?
- What biometrics use principles should be developed regarding contexts of operation, appropriate use guidelines, application domains, economic and social factors, and usability concerns? Are there domain-specific issues that arise (in connection with voting, e-commerce, large-crowd settings, or counterterrorism, for instance) that should be taken into account?
- How does due process enter into the policy framework for biometric systems?
- What approaches are courts likely to use in assessing the reliability of biometric evidence?

- From an economic perspective, how can government and private inputs and markets best be utilized to ensure the development of biometric technologies and human capital in this area?

Panelists:
Tora Bikson, RAND Corporation
David Kaye, Arizona State University
Lisa Nelson, University of Pittsburgh
Peter Swire, Ohio State University

6:30   Reception for committee and workshop participants

Wednesday, March 16

9:00 a.m.   Welcome back: Joe Pato

9:15-11:45   *Session 4: Scenarios and Applications*

Moderator: Gordon Levin

Potential Discussion Topics
- What characteristics have contributed to various biometric systems successes and failures? Are there any general lessons that can be learned?
- Are biometrics more or less appropriate for different application contexts (e.g., closed versus open systems, large versus small deployments, as password substitutes) and/or security environments (e.g., government versus commercial), and what characterizes those differences?
- What kind of threat models do different application contexts presume, and how are they dealt with?
- Have multibiometric fusion approaches been used successfully, and how might they be applied in the future?
- What strategies and approaches have been or are expected to be most successful in practice for overcoming biometric false rejection without compromising system security?
- What principles should be taken into account when determining how best to integrate biometrics into particular systems and/or environments?
- What role should training play for system users?

Panelists:
Joseph Atick, Identix
Rick Lazarick, Transportation Security Agency
Tony Mansfield, U.K. National Physical Laboratory
Cynthia Musselman, Authenti-Corp
Marek Rejman-Greene, British Telecommunications

11:45 a.m.-12:30 p.m.   Lunch

APPENDIX A   39

12:30-2:15   *Session 5: Information Sharing and Cooperation: Technical and Policy Aspects*

                    Moderator: Peter Higgins

                    Potential Discussion Topics
- What are the major challenges associated with "terrorist list" file sharing and aggregation, and how are they impacted or mitigated by the inclusion of biometrics?
- What are current biometric data-sharing activities, and to what extent have they been successful or unsuccessful (and why)?
- What should data policy look like in terms of database integration, data mining, and data privacy aspects in biometric system development and integration? What are the data policy implications of using and comparing biometrics data with other data sources? How does policy deal with sensitive but unclassified sources and methods as well as third-party ownership of biometric data (such as NATO countries providing fingerprints of terrorists to add to watch lists)?
- How is biometrics data- and information-sharing policy being shaped, and what should inform its development? What is missing from the national policy discussion that could facilitate the desired security objectives? If the issues center on legal policy, are they being addressed in a timely fashion or would a higher priority or higher-level legal authority help disposition of these issues?
- What is the role of your organization in international standards setting, forensics standards compliance, and cross-jurisdictional cooperation?

                    Panelists:
                    William Casey, Boston Police Department
                    Patty Cogswell and Neal Latta, US-VISIT
                    K.A. Taipale, Center for Advanced Studies in Science and Technology Policy
                    John Woodward, Department of Defense Biometrics Management Office, Biometrics Fusion Center

2:15-3:00   *Group Brainstorm* (This session did not take place due to lack of time; follow-up input in writing was solicited from participants.)

                    Moderator: Joe Pato

                    Potential Discussion Topics
- What are the important questions and issues that have come out of this workshop that the committee should seek to address in the rest of its study?
- Who should the committee be sure to hear from (individuals, groups, institutions, or areas of expertise)?
- How can this committee's work be most helpful to the broader community?

B

Biosketches of Committee Members and Staff

COMMITTEE MEMBERS

JOSEPH N. PATO, *Chair*, is a Distinguished Technologist at Hewlett-Packard's HP Laboratories, where he serves as lab scientist for the Trusted Systems Lab (TSL) and manager for TSL's Princeton research group. Previously he served as chief technology officer for Hewlett-Packard's Internet Security Solutions Division. Since 1986, Mr. Pato has been involved in security research and development, spending much of his career studying authentication, identification, and privacy issues. Currently Mr. Pato is developing a research program that will analyze security issues in the health care industry. Mr. Pato's current research focuses on the security needs of collaborative enterprises on the Internet, addressing both interenterprise models and the needs of lightweight instruments and peripherals directly attached to the Internet. Specifically, he is looking at critical infrastructure protection and the confluence of trust, e-services, and mobility. These interests have led him to look at the preservation of Internet communication in the event of cyberterrorism, trust frameworks for mobile environments, and how to apply privacy considerations in complex systems. His past work includes the design of delegation protocols for secure distributed computation, key exchange protocols, interdomain trust structures, the development of public- and secret-key-based infrastructures, and the more general development of distributed enterprise environments. Mr. Pato is also the founder of the IT-ISAC (IT Information Sharing and Analysis Center), where he also serves as a board member. Mr. Pato has participated on several standards or advisory committees of the Institute of Electrical and Electronics Engineers (IEEE), American National Standards Institute (ANSI), National Institute for Standards and Technology (NIST), Department of Commerce, W3C, Financial Services Technology Consortium (FSTC), and Common Open Software Environment (COSE). He has represented Hewlett-Packard to the Open Software Foundation (OSF) Architecture Planning Council, the technical arm of the OSF Board of Directors. He has also served on the Technical Planning Committee evolving the Distributed Computing Environment (DCE) and chaired the Security and Remote Procedure Call (RPC)/Programming Model/Environment Services working groups. He has served as the vice-chair for the Distributed Management Environment (DME)-DCE-Security working group of the OSF Security Special Interest Group. In the past, Mr. Pato served as the co-chair for the OASIS Security Services Technical Committee, which developed Security Assertions Markup Language (SAML) from June 2001 until November 2002. SAML 1.0 was approved as an OASIS standard on November 1, 2002. For the past 3 years, Mr. Pato has been an instructor at the Massachusetts Institute of Technology, teaching a course entitled Ethics and Law on the Electronic Frontier (electronic surveillance and copyright control). Mr. Pato served as a key member of CSTB's committee that wrote *Who Goes There? Authentication Through the Lens of Privacy* (2003). Mr. Pato's graduate work was in computer science at Brown University.

BOB BLAKLEY is chief scientist for security and privacy at IBM Tivoli Software. He was the general chair of the 2003 IEEE Security and Privacy Conference and served as general chair of the Association for Computing Machinery's (ACM's) New Security Paradigms Workshop. Dr. Blakley was a member of CSTB's committee that produced the report *Who Goes There? Authentication Through the Lens of Privacy* (2003). He was named Distinguished Security Practitioner by the 2002 ACM Computer Security and Applications Conference (ACSAC) and serves on the editorial board of the *International Journal of Information Security* (IJIS). He was the editor of the Object Management Group's (OMG's) CORBA security specification and is the author of *CORBA Security: An Introduction to Safe Computing with Objects*. Dr. Blakley was also the editor of the Open Group's Authorization API specification and the OASIS Security Services Technical Committee's SAML specification effort. He has been involved in cryptography and data security design work since 1979 and has authored or coauthored seven papers on cryptography, secret-sharing schemes, access control, and other aspects of computer security. He holds nine patents on security-related technologies. Dr. Blakley received an A.B. in classics from Princeton University and a master's degree and Ph.D. in computer and communications sciences from the University of Michigan.

JEANETTE BLOMBERG manages the Work in Organizational Context (WORC) group at the IBM Almaden Research Center. She joined IBM Research in 2002 to help establish Service Research, a group focused on providing research in support of IBM's Global Services division. Her research focuses on the interplay between people, technology, and organizational practices. Dr. Blomberg is also an industry-affiliated Professor of Human Work Science at the Blekinge Institute of Technology in Sweden, where she advises Ph.D. students and organizes a biennial Ph.D. course on work practice and design for students throughout the Nordic countries. Prior to assuming her current position at IBM, Dr. Blomberg was director of Experience Modeling Research at Sapient Corporation, where she helped establish the Experience Modeling practice and managed Sapient's San Francisco Experience Modeling group. While at Sapient she directed and participated in research projects for global technology, energy, automotive, transportation, consumer products, and financial services companies. Dr. Blomberg was also a founding member of the pioneering Work Practice and Technology group at the Xerox Palo Alto Research Center (PARC). Over the years her research has explored issues in social aspects of technology production and use, ethnographically informed organizational interventions, participatory design, case-based prototyping, and workplace studies. She received her Ph.D. in anthropology from the University of California, Davis, where she taught courses in cultural anthropology and sociolinguistics.

JOSEPH P. CAMPBELL received B.S., M.S., and Ph.D. degrees in electrical engineering from Rensselaer Polytechnic Institute in 1979, the Johns Hopkins University in 1986, and Oklahoma State University in 1992, respectively. Dr. Campbell is currently a senior member of the technical staff at the MIT Lincoln Laboratory in the Information Systems Technology Group, where he conducts speech-processing research and specializes in advanced speaker recognition methods. His current foci are high-level features for and forensic-style applications of speaker recognition, creating corpora to support speech-processing research and evaluation, robust speech coding, biometrics, and cognitive radio. Before joining Lincoln, he served 22 years at the National Security Agency (NSA). From 1979 to 1990, Dr. Campbell was a member of NSA's Narrowband Secure Voice Technology research group. He and his teammates developed the first DSP-chip software modem and LPC-10e, which enhanced the Federal Standard 1015 voice coder and improved U.S. and NATO secure voice systems. He was the principal investigator and led the U.S. government's speech coding team in developing the CELP voice coder, which became Federal Standard 1016 and is the foundation of digital cellular and voice-over-the-Internet telephony systems. From 1991 to 1998, Dr. Campbell was a senior scientist in NSA's Biometric Technology research group, where he led voice verification research. From 1994 to 1998, he chaired the Biometric Consortium, the U.S. government's focal point for research, development, test, evaluation, and application of biometric-based personal identification and verification technology. From 1998 to 2001, he led the Acoustics Section of NSA's Speech Research branch, conducting and coordinating research on and evaluation of speaker recognition, language identification, gender identification, and speech activity detection methods. From 1991 to 1999, Dr. Campbell was an associate editor of *IEEE Transactions on Speech and Audio Processing*. He was an IEEE Signal Processing Society Distinguished Lecturer in 2001. From 1991 to 2001, Dr. Campbell taught speech processing at the Johns Hopkins University. Dr. Campbell is currently a member of the IEEE Signal Processing Society's board of governors; an editor of *Digital Signal Processing* journal; a chair of the International Speech Communication Association's Speaker and Language Characterization Special Interest Group (ISCA SpLC SIG); a member of ISCA, Sigma Xi, and the Acoustical Society of America; and a fellow of the IEEE.

GEORGE T. DUNCAN is a professor of statistics in the H. John Heinz III School of Public Policy and Management and the Department of Statistics at Carnegie Mellon University. He was on the faculty of the University of California, Davis (1970-1974), and was a Peace Corps volunteer in the Philippines (1965-1967), teaching at Mindanao State University. His current research work centers on information technology and social accountability. He has published more than 50 papers in such journals as *Statistical Science, Management Science, Journal of the American Statistical Association, Econometrica,* and *Psychometrika.* He is a current and past recipient of National Science Foundation research funding and has lectured in Brazil, Italy, Turkey, Ireland, Mexico, and Japan, among other places. He chaired the Panel on Confidentiality and Data Access of the National Academy of Sciences (1989-1993), producing the report *Private Lives and Public Policies: Confidentiality and Accessibility of Government Statistics.* He chaired the American Statistical Association's Committee on Privacy and Confidentiality. He is a fellow of the American Statistical Association, an elected member of the International Statistical Institute, and a fellow of the American Association for the Advancement of Science. In 1996 he was elected Pittsburgh Statistician of the Year by the American Statistical Association. He has been editor of the Theory and Methods Section of the *Journal of the American Statistical Association.* He received a B.S. (1963) and an M.S. (1964) from the University of Chicago and a Ph.D. (1970) from the University of Minnesota, all in the field of statistics.

DELORES ETTER is a professor in the Department of Electrical Engineering at the U.S. Naval Academy. Dr. Etter joined the electrical engineering faculty at the United States Naval Academy in August 2001 as the first recipient of the Office of Naval Research Distinguished Chair in Science and Technology. From 1998 to 2001, Dr. Etter served as the Deputy Under Secretary of Defense for Science and Technology. In that position, she was responsible for the Defense Science and Technology strategic planning, budget allocation, program execution, and evaluation for the Department of Defense science and technology program. Prior to that she was a tenured professor in electrical and computer engineering at the University of Colorado from 1990 to 1998 and at the University of New Mexico (UNM) from 1979 to 1989. In 1998, she served as associate vice president for academic affairs at UNM. She also spent a year in the Electrical Engineering Department of Stanford University as a visiting professor in the Information Systems Laboratory. Dr. Etter is a member of the National Academy of Engineering and the National Science Board. Her research interests are in biometrics and digital signal processing. She is also the author of a number of textbooks on computer languages and software engineering.

GEORGE R. FISHER is formerly a chief administrative officer for Prudential-Wachovia, where he led the merger of Prudential Securities into Wachovia in 2002. Prior to joining Prudential, Mr. Fisher was chief information officer at Fidelity Investments, where he managed technology oversight, consolidating mutual fund and brokerage platforms. Mr. Fisher also spent 16 years at Morgan Stanley, first as a principal for Technical Services Worldwide, transforming manual, low-volume systems into Wall Street leaders; later he became managing director of finance, administration, and operations for Morgan Stanley Asia, restructuring Chinese operations and managing the explosive growth of Asia's regional markets. He also oversaw the first audit of a foreign securities firm by the Japanese Ministry of Finance. Mr. Fisher earned a B.A. in economics and computer science from the University of Rochester. He has also earned certifications from the National Association of Securities Dealers (Series 3, 7, 63, 24, and 27), the National Association of Corporate Directors (Director of Professionalism), the American Chamber of Commerce in Japan, and the Association of International Education of Japan, earning Level 4 language proficiency.

STEVEN P. GOLDBERG is a professor of law at the Georgetown University Law Center. An expert in law and science, Mr. Goldberg is the author of *Culture Clash: Law and Science in America* (1996), winner of the Alpha Sigma Nu Book Award, and coauthor of the widely used text *Law, Science, and Medicine*. He served as a law clerk to D.C. Circuit Court Chief Judge David L. Bazelon and U.S. Supreme Court Justice William J. Brennan, Jr. He also served as an attorney in the General Counsel's Office of the U.S. Nuclear Regulatory Commission. Mr. Goldberg is a member of the D.C. and Maryland bars and the Section on Science and Technology of the American Bar Association. He received his A.B. from Harvard College and his J.D. from Yale Law School.

PETER T. HIGGINS, founder of Higgins & Associates, International (which he recently merged with ASCG of Nevada to form the Higgins-Hermansen Group, LLC), has 35 years' experience in the information technology field and has been involved with biometrics since the late 1980s. He is an instructor of biometrics at the University of California, Los Angeles, Extension School. He chaired the International Association for Identification's AFIS Committee for 5 years and is a well-known consultant in the field of large-scale biometric procurement and testing. In 2002 he joined John Woodward and Nick Orlans in authoring the McGraw-Hill/Osborne book *Biometric Identification in the Information Age*. Previously he served as deputy assistant director of engineering with the FBI and was the program manager for the FBI's Integrated Automated Fingerprint Identification System (IAFIS). Prior to this he served in technical, operational, and executive positions with the Central Intelligence Agency. Mr. Higgins received a B.A. in mathematics from Marist College and an M.S. in theoretical math and computer science from Stevens Institute of Technology in Hoboken, New Jersey.

PETER B. IMREY is a member of the Cleveland Clinic Department of Quantitative Health Sciences, teaches in the Clinic's Lerner College of Medicine of Case Western Reserve University, and is affiliate professor in the Department of Statistics, University of Illinois at Urbana-Champaign. He previously served on the faculties of the Universities of North Carolina (Biostatistics, 1972-1975) and Illinois (Medical Information Science; Statistics; and Community Health, 1975-2002). Dr. Imrey has made research and expository contributions to statistical analysis of categorical data and to diverse health science areas, including meningococcal disease, diet and cancer, and dental data analysis. He has served on editorial boards of three statistical journals and the *Encyclopedia of Biostatistics* (2nd edition), on numerous federal special study sections and emphasis panels, and on the National Academies' committee that produced the report *The Polygraph and Lie Detection* (2003). He has also held major elective posts in the American Statistical Association, the American Public Health Association (APHA), and the International Biometric Society (IBS), including 2005 president of the IBS Eastern North American Region. Dr. Imrey has been honored by APHA's Statistics Section, and is a fellow of the American College of Epidemiology and a member of Sigma Xi and Delta Omega honorary societies. He received his A.B. in mathematics and statistics from

Columbia University and his Ph.D. in biostatistics from the University of North Carolina at Chapel Hill.

ANIL K. JAIN is a University Distinguished Professor in the Department of Computer Science and Engineering at Michigan State University and was the department chair from 1995 to 1999. His research interests include statistical pattern recognition, exploratory pattern analysis, Markov random fields, texture analysis, three-dimensional object recognition, medical image analysis, document image analysis, and biometric authentication. He received the best paper awards in 1987 and 1991 and was cited for outstanding contributions in 1976, 1979, 1992, 1997, and 1998 from the Pattern Recognition Society. He also received the 1996 IEEE Transactions on Neural Networks Outstanding Paper Award. He is a fellow of the IEEE, the ACM, and the International Association of Pattern Recognition (IAPR). He was the editor in chief of the IEEE Transactions on Pattern Analysis and Machine Intelligence (1991-1994). He has received a Fulbright Research Award, a Guggenheim fellowship, and the Alexander von Humboldt Research Award. Dr. Jain delivered the 2002 Pierre Devijver lecture sponsored by the IAPR. He holds six patents in the area of fingerprint matching and has written or edited three books on biometrics: *Handbook of Face Recognition; Handbook of Fingerprint Recognition;* and *Biometrics: Personal Identification in Networked Society*. Dr. Jain was the co-organizer of the NSF workshop on the biometrics research agenda, held in May 2003, and has organized several conferences on biometrics. He received a Ph.D. in electrical engineering from Ohio State University in 1973.

GORDON LEVIN is senior engineer with the Advanced Systems group of Design and Engineering at Walt Disney World in Orlando, where the world's largest commercial biometric application has been operating since 1997. As a licensed electrical engineer, he is the engineer of record for all physical security system design performed on the 42-square-mile property. Mr. Levin has been a member of the Biometric Consortium Working Group (BCWG) since 1999 and the sole commercial end user to be a participating representative acting under NIST and the NSA to incubate biometric standards for submission to ANSI and the International Organization for Standardization (ISO). In 2002 he was the keynote speaker at the plenary meeting of ISO/IEC Joint Technical Committee 1 Subcommittee 37 on Biometrics. He also participated in the Aviation Security–Biometrics Working Group that was assembled in the wake of 9/11 to report on passenger protection and identity verification. This report was instrumental in the strategic planning for the soon-to-be-formed Transportation Security Administration (TSA) and its plans for adopting biometric technology. Prior to joining Walt Disney World in 1997, Mr. Levin had been a private consultant engineer working in the DOD and commercial sectors in specialized security and electronic system design and construction.

LAWRENCE D. NADEL is a fellow at the Center for Information and Telecommunications Technologies at Mitretek Systems. His current focus is on the requirements for and issues associated with implementing effective and interoperable biometric identification and authentication systems and objective methods for testing and evaluating the performance of these systems. He has provided technical leadership to a variety of national identification and security-related projects for agencies such as the TSA (Airport Access Control Pilot Program), the Department of Defense Biometric Management Office, and the FBI (IAFIS and the Universal Latent Workstation). Dr. Nadel has supported state and local law enforcement and the National Institute of Justice through Mitretek's Center for Criminal Justice Technology (reference ballistic imaging, the impact of biometric encoded drivers' licenses on law enforcement, and biometric-based identification credentials for criminal justice and public safety officials). He is coprincipal investigator on a Mitretek-funded research project to assess and develop biometric fusion methods. He chairs Mitretek's Biometric

Identification Cluster Group, is Mitretek's tech lead for biometrics, and is a participant in the INCITS-M1 biometrics standards group. He earned a B.S. degree in electrical engineering from Polytechnic University and M.Sc. and Ph.D. degrees in electrical and biomedical engineering from Ohio State University.

JAMES L. WAYMAN is a senior fellow and director of the biometric identification research program of the San Jose State University Research Institute. He served as director of the U.S. National Biometric Test Center in the Clinton administration (1997-2000). He holds four patents in speech processing and is a "principal U.K. expert" (PUKE) on the ISO/IEC standards committee biometrics. Dr. Wayman is a senior member of the IEEE. He was a member of CSTB's committee that produced *Who Goes There? Authentication Through the Lens of Privacy*. Dr. Wayman received his Ph.D. degree in engineering from the University of California, Santa Barbara, in 1980.

STAFF

LYNETTE I. MILLETT is a senior program officer and study director at the Computer Science and Telecommunications Board of the National Academies. She is currently involved in several CSTB projects, including a comprehensive exploration of privacy in the information age, a study on certification and dependable software systems, an assessment of the Social Security Administration's E-Government Strategy, and an activity on biometrics technologies, among other things. Ms. Millett recently completed a small activity on the topic of radio-frequency identification technologies. She also recently completed a CSTB project that produced *Who Goes There? Authentication Technologies and Their Privacy Implications* and *IDs—Not That Easy: Questions About Nationwide Identity Systems*. Before joining CSTB, she worked on static analysis techniques for concurrent programming languages as well as research on value-sensitive design and informed consent online. She has an M.Sc. in computer science from Cornell University along with a B.A. in mathematics and computer science with honors from Colby College. Her graduate work was supported by both an NSF graduate fellowship and an Intel graduate fellowship.

KRISTEN BATCH is an associate program officer with CSTB. She is involved with projects focusing on wireless communication technologies and the work of the Whither Biometrics committee. While pursuing an M.A. in international communications from American University, she interned at the National Telecommunications and Information Administration, in the Office of International Affairs, and at the Center for Strategic and International Studies, in the Technology and Public Policy Program. She earned a B.A. from Carnegie Mellon University in literary and cultural studies and Spanish and received two travel grants to conduct independent research in Spain.

MARGARET MARSH HUYNH, senior program assistant, has been with CSTB since January 1999 supporting several projects. She is currently supporting the projects Wireless Technology Prospects and Policy and Whither Biometrics. She previously worked on the projects that produced *Signposts in Cyberspace: The Domain Name System and Internet Navigation; Getting Up to Speed: The Future of Supercomputing; Beyond Productivity: Information Technology, Innovation, and Creativity; IT Roadmap to a Geospatial Future; Building a Workforce for the Information Economy*; and *The Digital Dilemma: Intellectual Property in the Information Age*. Ms. Huynh also assisted with the project Exploring Information Technology Issues for the Behavioral and Social Sciences (digital divide and democracy). She assists on other projects as needed. Before coming to the National Academies, Ms. Huynh worked as a meeting assistant at Management for Meetings, April to August 1998, and as a meeting assistant at the American Society for Civil Engineers from September 1996 to

April 1998. Ms. Huynh has a B.A. (1990) in liberal studies, with minors in sociology and psychology from Salisbury University.

What Is CSTB?

As a part of the National Research Council, the Computer Science and Telecommunications Board (CSTB) was established in 1986 to provide independent advice to the federal government on technical and public policy issues relating to computing and communications. Composed of leaders from industry and academia, CSTB conducts studies of critical national issues and makes recommendations to government, industry, and academia. CSTB also provides a neutral meeting ground for consideration of complex issues where resolution and action may be premature. It convenes discussions that bring together principals from the public and private sectors, ensuring consideration of key perspectives. The majority of CSTB's work is requested by federal agencies and Congress, consistent with its National Academies' context.

A pioneer in framing and analyzing Internet policy issues, CSTB is unique in its comprehensive scope and its effective, interdisciplinary appraisal of technical, economic, social, and policy issues. Beginning with early work in computer and communications security, cyber-assurance and information systems trustworthiness have been cross-cutting themes in CSTB's work. CSTB has produced several reports that have become classics in the field, and it continues to address these topics as they grow in importance.

To do its work, CSTB draws on some of the best minds in the country and from around the world, inviting experts to participate in its projects as a public service. Studies are conducted by balanced committees without direct financial interests in the topics they are addressing. Those committees meet, confer electronically, and build analyses through their deliberations. Additional expertise is tapped in a rigorous process of review and critique, further enhancing the quality of CSTB reports. By engaging groups of principals, CSTB gets the facts and insights critical to assessing key issues.

The mission of CSTB is to

- Respond to requests from the government, nonprofit organizations, and private industry for advice on computer and telecommunications issues and from the government for advice on computer and telecommunications systems planning, utilization, and modernization.
- Monitor and promote the health of the fields of computer science and telecommunications, with attention to issues of human resources, information infrastructure, and societal impacts.
- Initiate and conduct studies involving computer science, technology, and telecommunications as critical resources.
- Foster interaction among the disciplines underlying computing and telecommunications technologies and other fields, at large and within the National Academies.

CSTB projects address a diverse range of topics affected by the evolution of information technology. Recently completed reports include *Who Goes There? Authentication Through the Lens of Privacy*; *The Internet Under Crisis Conditions: Learning from September 11*; *Cybersecurity Today and Tomorrow: Pay Now or Pay Later*; *Youth, Pornography, and the Internet*; *Broadband: Bringing Home the Bits*; and *Innovation in Information Technology*. For further information about CSTB reports and active projects, see <http://cstb.org>.